SAT Essay: Red

Homework: Version 1.3

C2 Education is a registered trademark of C2 Educational Center, Inc.

This publication is designed to provide accurate and authoritative information in regard to the subject matter covered. It is sold with the understanding that the publisher is not engaged in rendering legal, accounting, or other professional service. If legal advice or other expert assistance is required, the services of a competent professional should be sought.

© 2013 by Reetiforp, LLC. All rights reserved. Printed in the United States of America. Except as permitted under the United States Copyright Act of 1976, no part of this publication may be reproduced or distributed in any form or by any means, or stored in a data base or retrieval system, without the prior written permission of the publisher.

Published by Reetiforp, LLC Publishing, a division of Reetiforp, LLC

Reetiforp Publishing books are available at special quantity discounts to use for sales promotions, employee premiums, or educational purposes. Please email our Marketing Department to order or for more information at c2educate@c2educate.com. Please report any errors or corrections to c2tutors@c2educate.com.

SAT Essay Red: Table of Contents

Page	Red Essay
1	**Red Essay 1: SAT Essay Basics**
7	Homework
11	**Red Essay 2: Analyzing the Topic**
18	Homework
21	**Red Essay 3: Brainstorming the Essay**
29	Homework
33	**Red Essay 4: Planning the Essay**
44	Homework
46	**Red Essay 5: Improving Your Examples**
53	Homework
56	**Red Essay 6: Paragraph Organization**
64	Homework
67	**Red Essay 7: The Art of Persuasion**
74	Homework
77	**Red Essay 8: Conclusions and Instructions**
84	Homework
87	**Red Essay 9: Adding Flair**
94	Homework
97	**Red Essay 10: Editing**
101	Homework
103-202	**Practice Essays 11-30**

Red Essay 1

SAT Essay Basics

The College Board added the writing portion to the SAT in 2005 because many colleges complained about the lack of examples of a student's writing ability. The writing section, worth 800 points of the total test score, is made up of two parts: The essay and the multiple choice sections. The multiple choice counts for roughly 70% of your total writing score – the rest of your score is based on the essay.

This means that a perfect essay score could count for almost 170 points of your overall SAT score.

Even if you've read the College Board website, it can be very difficult to figure out exactly what the essay graders are looking for in a "perfect" essay. Because the College Board's essay grading rubric is very vague, there doesn't seem to be a simple checklist of things an essay must have in order to receive a six.

In the space below, make a list of things that you think an SAT essay has to have in order to receive a perfect score.

- _____
- _____
- _____
- _____
- _____
- _____

The Very Basic SAT Essay

Essay graders look at 5 basic components when they decide on your essay score: Thesis statement, supporting details, organization, grammar/spelling, and diction/word choice.

There are several basic things that the essay graders look for first. Essays which have these basic requirements should receive at least a 3 or 4 out of 6. The most very basic requirements are:

- **Thesis Statement/Position:**
    - Include a thesis statement.
    - Put it in your introduction.
    - Clearly state your position and make sure that it is *on the given topic*.
- **Supporting Details/Examples:**
    - Have at least 2 specific examples.
    - Don't use imaginary/hypothetical examples.
    - Explain your examples clearly and logically.
- **Organization:**
    - At least one page of writing, if not more.
    - More than 1 paragraph – preferably 4 or more.
    - Essays should include an introduction, body paragraphs, and a conclusion.
- **Grammar/Spelling:**
    - Avoid having grammar/spelling errors.
    - Never let errors interfere with the reader's ability to understand.
- **Diction/Word Choice:**
    - No inappropriate language.
    - No slang.
    - An attempt at sophisticated word choice.

Because you are studying at the Red level, you should already be including all of these things in your essays. If you need to review any information about any of these grading areas, you should go back and review the information in the Blue level for essay writing.

These basic requirements are the most fundamental components of an SAT essay. If you want to score above the three to four range – if you want that perfect essay score – you need to go *a lot* further than these requirements.

Which of these grading areas do you have the most trouble with? What do you think you need to do to improve your score in that area?

_____
_____
_____
_____
_____
_____
_____

Going Above and Beyond: The Perfect Score

To get a perfect 6 on the SAT essay, you will need to go above and beyond the basic essay requirements. Some of the things that a perfect essay should include are:

- **Insight:** A perfect essay will demonstrate the writer's critical thinking skills. The writer may have a unique point of view on the topic, or the writer might include a creative persuasive argument; no matter how this insight is displayed, it will be clear to the reader that the writer has given great thought to his reasoning and arguments.
- **SEVERAL Well Developed Examples:** To receive a perfect score, an essay must include *at least* 2 – though 3 would be much better – very well explained and well argued examples. These examples ought to come from different sources (not all from history, or all from your personal experiences). For each example, you should fully explain the example and exactly *how* it supports and proves your argument.
- **Tight organizational structure that flows throughout the essay:** A "perfect" essay is not only very well organized, but also easy and enjoyable to read. This means that it must flow from one sentence or paragraph to the next without any awkward pauses or phrasing. This also means using strong transitions – going beyond the basic "first, second, in conclusion" to create a good flow from one thought to the next.
- **Sophisticated use of language:** The entire purpose of the SAT essay is to determine whether you have a skill with written language. To display these skills, you will want to include "sophisticated language choices": varied word choice, varied sentence structure, strong and vivid descriptions, and a few choice "$5" words.

Which of these things do you think will be the most challenging for you to include in your essay? What do you think you can do to improve in this area?

Common Essay Problems

Our essay graders have identified several common problems among SAT essays. These are problems that many students have, but which you will need to overcome in order to earn that elusive high score!

- **Quality over Quantity:** Many more advanced students tend to value quality over quantity in their writing. In the real world, this is great! But it is important to realize that the SAT essay is unlike any other writing assignment you will ever have, largely because the people grading the essays are forced to grade them very quickly and therefore cannot read the essays in great depth. On the SAT essay, 2 semi-well explained examples will generally receive a higher score than 1 very well explained example; while you should always strive for quality, quantity is also important!
- **Flat Writing:** Flat writing is writing that seems mass produced. This includes things such as thesis statements which are simple restatements of the essay prompt, overly used transitions such as "first" or "in conclusion", or clichéd phrases and statements. Such writing shows a basic understanding of essay writing, but does not show any particular skill or facility with language.
- **Part of an Excellent Essay:** Time management is essential on the SAT essay. Too many students write excellent partial essays and run out of time before they can finish. You will be better off writing a slightly less than perfect – but complete! – essay than writing only part of a really excellent essay.

Have you ever had trouble with one of these problems? If yes, explain. If no, identify another problem that you have had on the SAT essay. What do you think you can do to avoid this problem in the future?

_____
_____
_____
_____
_____
_____
_____
_____
_____
_____
_____
_____
_____
_____

Time Management

Your mission, should you choose to accept it (and let's face it: you don't have much of a choice), is to craft a complete, well argued, well organized, and fully edited essay in 25 minutes or less.

Sound tough? We promise: it's not. Once you develop a step by step procedure for writing a timed essay and familiarize yourself with the essay writing process, you will be able to crank out a 25 minute essay in your sleep. It's all a matter practice.

For many students, it is the short time limit that poses the biggest hurdle. These students often choose to skip the writing process and spend the entire time period writing, hoping that this will allow greater time to craft a strong essay.

WRONG.

Even though you only have a few short minutes to write the essay, you should still follow most of the steps of the writing process:

Read/analyze/understand the topic	1 minute
Brainstorm examples and outline essay	5 minutes
Write the essay	17 minutes
Revise/edit the essay	2 minutes

Step One: Read/analyze/understand the topic, 1 minute

Take just one minute to read the essay prompt, make sure you understand the question you are being asked, and analyze the topic so that you can begin prewriting. Taking this time to really examine the essay prompt makes it easier to brainstorm examples and plan your essay.

Step Two: Brainstorm examples and outline essay, 5 minutes

Take no more than 5 minutes to jot down as many examples as you can, decide which position to take in your essay, and write a very brief outline showing how you will organize your essay. This might sound like a waste of time, but it will not only speed up the writing process, it will also help you write a clearer and more organized essay.

Step Three: Write the essay, 17 minutes

This step is pretty self-explanatory: write the essay. Use your outline to help you organize your thoughts; as long as you follow your outline, the essay itself should come fairly naturally. You should take up most of your time writing the essay, but be sure to leave yourself a minute or two at the end to read it over and edit it!

Step Four: Revise/edit the essay, 1 minute

Always leave yourself a minute or two at the end to read your essay over and correct any errors, misspelled words, awkward phrases, repetitive language, or other minor issues. You would be amazed how many problems you can fix by simply taking a moment to read your essay over before your time is up. Because the essay is intended to show your skill with language, it is important that you take the time to catch any errors!

Use the space below to explain your current essay writing procedure. What do you do, step-by-step, when you sit down to write a timed SAT essay? How does your method differ from the one we've just explained? Do you think that the "C2" method will help you? Why or why not?

HOMEWORK

Use the following pages to plan and write an essay on the following essay prompt. You will not be timed, but you should try to follow the time table described in this lesson. When you have finished writing your essay, use the space provided to describe any difficulties you had in following the essay writing steps.

> Think carefully about the issue presented in the following excerpt and the assignment below:
>
> > If you rest, you rust.
> >
> > ~Helen Hayes
>
> **Assignment:** Do you agree that those who fail to strive regress? Plan and write an essay in which you develop your point of view on this issue. Support your position with reasoning and examples taken from your reading, studies, experience, or observations.

Which part of the writing process did you have the most difficulty with?

What can you do to improve?

Red Essay 2

Analyzing the Topic

An SAT essay prompt has three parts:

1. The excerpt: The quote or passage used to introduce the actual writing assignment
2. The assignment: This is where the actual question is asked. Sometimes the question is straightforward and simple, and other times you will need to do a bit of analysis to fully understand exactly what you are being asked.
3. The instructions: The instructions will always remain the same for every single essay. You should take time to read them now so that you don't need to waste time with them on the actual SAT.

The only part of the essay prompt that you *absolutely positively MUST* pay very close attention to is the assignment. **In order to avoid an automatic zero on your essay, you must be sure to identify and answer the question being asked!**

We suggest that you read the assignment first, and then read the excerpt. Once you know what you are being asked, you will likely have a more useful point of view as you read the excerpt.

You should never, ever use the excerpt as part of your essay – the excerpt is given to you, and the graders already know what it says, so you should not include it in your essay. However, the excerpt can be useful:

- **When the question asks whether you agree with the ideas in the excerpt**: Obviously, if the question asks if you agree with the excerpt, you will need to read and think about the excerpt in order to form your answer.
- **When you have trouble figuring out what the question is really asking**: If you cannot figure out what the core issue of the question is, you might find it helpful to read and consider the excerpt. The excerpt almost always offers a view or opinion about the central idea of the essay question. It might provide you with the inspiration you need to get started planning your essay.
- **When you have trouble deciding on a position**: If you have trouble picking a side, you might find the excerpt helpful. Usually, the excerpt will take a position on the topic; the position in the excerpt might inspire you and allow you to determine your own position on the topic.
- **When you're just plain stuck**: Again, the excerpt may be able to provide you with just enough inspiration to get started. If you find yourself at a loss as to what to write in your essay, sometimes the excerpt may prove helpful.

Analyzing the Topic: Step by Step

By taking a deep look at the topic right away, you will make planning and writing your essay much easier. As you read and consider the topic, you will "jump start" the brainstorming process, gearing your mind up to begin thinking about the direction your essay will go in. Most importantly, thoroughly considering the topic will help you to come up with a more unique thesis statement, which is arguably the most important single sentence in your essay.

To analyze the topic, follow these simple steps:

1. Locate the question.
2. Rephrase the question using your own words.
3. Summarize the excerpt in your own words.

Example:

> Think carefully about the issue presented in the following excerpt and the assignment below:
>
> If you rest, you rust.
>
> ~Helen Hayes
>
> **Assignment:** <u>Do you agree that those who fail to strive regress?</u> Plan and write an essay in which you develop your point of view on this issue. Support your position with reasoning and examples taken from your reading, studies, experience, or observations.

Reword the Question: *Do people who stop trying to achieve success lose valuable skills, knowledge, or other tools?*

Summarize the Excerpt: *If you stop trying, you lose ground.*

Why Bother?

By identifying the question, you will ensure that your essay addresses the question being asked. This is the only way to be certain that you essay is on topic – *off topic essays receive an automatic ZERO.*

By rewording the question, you make it easier to come up with a strong thesis statement. This eliminates the temptation to simply rephrase the original essay question, what we call a "cookie-cutter" thesis. If you answer your rewritten question instead, you will still be addressing the essay prompt but you won't be recycling the exact same language.

By summarizing the excerpt, you give yourself a starting point for your brainstorming. The excerpt can help you if you get stuck while planning and writing your essay, so it's almost always a good idea to spend a moment or two thinking about what the excerpt is saying.

Practice with Topics

For each of the following essay prompts, underline the question being asked, put the question into your own words, and then summarize the excerpt.

1. > Think carefully about the issue presented in the following excerpt and assignment below:
  >
  > If a man is called to be a street sweeper, he should sweep streets even as Michelangelo painted, or Beethoven composed music, or Shakespeare wrote poetry. He should sweep streets so well that all the hosts of heaven and earth will pause to say, here lived a great street sweeper who did his job well.
  > ~Martin Luther King, Jr.
  >
  > **Assignment:** Should you take pride in any job you have or only those jobs which carry a high status? Plan and write an essay in which you develop your point of view on this issue. Support your position with reasoning and examples taken from your reading, studies, experience, or observations.

Reword the Question: _____
_____
_____

Summarize the Excerpt: _____
_____
_____

2. > Think carefully about the issue presented in the following excerpt and assignment below:
  >
  > All animals, except man, know that the principle business of life is to enjoy it.
  > ~Samuel Butler
  >
  > **Assignment:** Is having fun a key part of life or a waste of valuable time? Plan and write an essay in which you develop your point of view on this issue. Support your position with reasoning and examples taken from your reading, studies, experience, or observations.

Reword the Question: _____
_____
_____

Summarize the Excerpt: _____
_____
_____

3.

> Think carefully about the issue presented in the following excerpt and assignment below:
>
> > The greater danger for most lies not in setting our aim too high and falling short, but in setting our aim too low and achieving our mark.
> > ~Michelangelo
>
> **Assignment:** Is it better to risk failure while attempting something ambitious or to succeed at something you were already certain you could achieve? Plan and write an essay in which you develop your point of view on this issue. Support your position with reasoning and examples taken from your reading, studies, experience, or observations.

Reword the Question: _____
_____
_____

Summarize the Excerpt: _____
_____
_____

> Think carefully about the issue presented in the following excerpt and assignment below:
>
> > Treating your adversary with respect is giving him an advantage to which he is not entitled.
> > ~Samuel Johnson
>
> **Assignment:** Is it poor strategy to respect one's opponents? Plan and write an essay in which you develop your point of view on this issue. Support your position with reasoning and examples taken from your reading, studies, experience, or observations.

Reword the Question: _____
_____
_____

Summarize the Excerpt: _____
_____
_____

Insightful Writing Starts with the Prompt

As we mentioned in lesson 1, one of the most important things for you to include in your essays in order to achieve a very high score is **insight**.

Insight (noun):

1. The ability to see clearly and intuitively into the nature of a complex subject
2. A clear perception and understanding of something

Use the space provided below to explain how insight can help to improve the overall quality of an essay.

_____
_____
_____
_____
_____
_____
_____
_____
_____
_____
_____
_____
_____
_____

When we say that you need to write an *insightful* essay, what do we mean?

First, we expect you to treat the essay topic as a complex issue. Too often, students will offer a simple yes or no answer to the essay question. While you do have to take a firm stance on the topic, you should take the time to recognize that any essay topic is a complex issue which might have a multitude of potential answers. In other words, no SAT essay topic exists in black and white – there are always shades of gray. It is important that you recognize these shades of gray in your essay. Some tips:

- **Don't use absolutes.** Avoid saying things like, "It is always better to do this than that" or "All people should do this." Absolutes are rarely true, especially when dealing with issues such as those that come up on the SAT essay. They are overly simplistic and suggest a poor understanding of the topic at hand.
- **Recognize the opposition.** Let's say that you are writing an essay about why you feel that technology has been beneficial to society. You might include a paragraph about why others might feel that technology has been harmful to society, and then refute the argument. For example: "Many people feel that technology has posed many harms to society, suggesting that many of our modern technologies have caused people to lose focus and become easily distracted. However, although certain technologies may have encouraged poor concentration in some people, the fact remains that technology in general has helped us to create a more productive and efficient

workforce than ever before." By doing this, you are recognizing the opposing opinion and then explaining why this opinion is wrong. This shows that you understand both sides of the argument, which suggests that your opinion is well thought out.
- **Don't oversimplify.** This doesn't mean that you have to address every nuance or mini-issue of the topic, but you should clearly show that you recognize that the issue is not a straightforward one.

Secondly, an insightful essay is one which shows a clear understanding of the topic. This is part of the reason why it is important to take the time to truly analyze the topic. Many students will offer a strange interpretation of the excerpt or the topic itself which shows an obvious lack of understanding regarding the essay prompt. In your essay, you need to show that you clearly understood the question you were asked. Some tips:

- **Don't reference confusion.** If the excerpt is at all confusing to you, *don't use it, talk about it, or reference it in your essay*. Stick to what you DO understand and avoid what you don't. If the question itself confuses you, then keep rewording it until you find a phrasing which you can easily understand.
- **Narrow down a broad topic.** If the topic seems too broad, or if the topic seems to include issues that you do not fully understand, then you should narrow the topic down to make it more manageable.

Review What You've Learned

Answer each of the following questions using complete sentences.

1. What are the four steps that you should always follow when writing an SAT essay?

2. Why is it important to identify the question being asked in the essay prompt?

3. How can the excerpt help you with your essay?

4. Why is it important to analyze the essay prompt?

5. What are some ways to include insight in your essay?

HOMEWORK

Use the following pages to plan and write an essay on the following essay prompt. You will not be timed, but you should try to follow the time table described in this lesson. When you have finished writing your essay, use the space provided to describe any difficulties you had in following the essay writing steps.

> Think carefully about the issue presented in the following excerpt and the assignment below:
>
> Progress is not an illusion, it happens, but it is slow and invariably disappointing.
>
> ~George Orwell
>
> **Assignment:** Do you agree that rapid progress is not possible? Plan and write an essay in which you develop your point of view on this issue. Support your position with reasoning and examples taken from your reading, studies, experience, or observations.

Reword the Question:

_____

_____

Summarize the Excerpt:

_____

_____

Red Essay 3

Brainstorming the Essay

Let Your Examples Be Your Guide

Once you have analyzed the topic and you fully understand the question you are supposed to answer, it's time to figure out exactly what your answer will be. The might sound simple enough: You are asked to develop your point of view, so you should answer with your opinion. WRONG.

Regardless of what your personal opinion is on a given topic, you should always let your examples guide you in forming your answer.

For a lot of SAT topics, it is much easier to quickly come up with examples for one side than another. Even if you disagree with the position your examples support, writing a timed essay will be much easier if you adapt your position to fit your examples than if you try to come up with examples that fit your position.

Instead, we suggest that you jot down as many examples as you can think of, regardless of which position they support. Then, once you have a list of examples, decide which examples you will use and which position they support. This accomplishes two tasks:

- Helps you to know exactly what you will include in your essay, which makes writing the actual essay faster and easier.
- Forces you to consider both sides of the issue, which will help you to include insight in your essay.

This means that the first step of brainstorming for your essay will be to come up with as many examples as you can in a very short period of time. You want to aim for about five or six potential examples, but you shouldn't spend more than two or three minutes coming up with them!

When writing an SAT essay, do you usually decide your position and then come up with examples, or do you come up with examples and then decide your position? Why do you do this? What are some benefits of your method?

_____
_____
_____
_____
_____
_____
_____
_____
_____
_____

For example:

> Think carefully about the issue presented in the following excerpt and the assignment below:
>
> > A new scientific truth does not triumph by convincing its opponents and making them see the light, but rather its opponents eventually die, and a new generation grows up familiar with it.   ~Max Planck
>
> **Assignment:** Do you agree that people have difficulty accepting new and unfamiliar ideas? Plan and write an essay in which you develop your point of view on this issue. Support your position with reasoning and examples taken from your reading, studies, experience, or observations.

Reword the Question: *Do people tend to resist new thoughts and opinions?*

Brainstorm Examples:

- *resist* 1. *Racism/Civil Rights Movement: Much opposition to giving blacks equality, took decades to really reach equality*
- *no* 2. *Modern Technology: Seems that newer is always better, people have no trouble with new stuff*
- *resist* 3. *Galileo: Challenged the Church and promoted the theory that the Earth moved around the Sun; was convicted for heresy.*
- *no* 4. *Research and Development: Countries spend billions supporting scientific research to come up with new ideas, new ideas are desired not feared*
- *resist* 5. *Educating women: For hundreds of years, women were not allowed to be educated; today it is common place, but it took many decades for this change to occur*

Look at the examples the writer has come up with. What position do you think the writer should take in his essay? Which examples do you think he should use?

People tend to resist new thoughts. 1,3,5

All Examples Are Not Created Equal

You should think of your examples as evidence – the better your evidence, the stronger your arguments. To write a good persuasive essay, you should always use strong, concrete examples.

What are some types of examples that you think are strong? What makes these examples strong?

Specific examples because they have ground hypothetical ideas in reality.

A strong example is one that is most likely to persuade your reader to agree with you. In your essay, you will be trying to PROVE that you are right – your examples are your proof. When you are deciding which examples to use, you will want to consider the source of each example.

Look at the following pairs of examples. All of these examples are good, but some are better than others. In each pair, circle the example that you think is more persuasive. Then use the space provided to briefly explain why you think that example is the more persuasive example.

1. Topic: Luck is not necessary for success.
    a. As a freshman, I had trouble with some of my classes. When I really focused on my schoolwork, my grades improved. Luck had nothing to do with this success, hard work did.
    b. When Thomas Edison set out to invent the light bulb, he failed hundreds of times before finally succeeding. In the end, he did not achieve success through luck but through persistence and intelligence.

Why? *Thomas Edison's example takes the writer's idea + gives a real life example*

2. Topic: It is the little things in life that matter most.
    a. A recent study shows that, beyond a certain income point, additional money does not result in greater happiness. Instead, the study found that things such as job satisfaction and close family ties had a much greater impact on people's happiness than things such as wealth or status. In other words, money really can't buy happiness because happiness comes from the "little" things in life.
    b. Although Bill Gates is among the richest men in the world, after he retired from actively running Microsoft he said that he would find much more happiness in doing charitable work and helping others than in working to make more money. Even the richest man in the world finds greater happiness in the "little" things than in money.

Why? _____

3. Topic: Deception can be justified.
   a. When a pharmaceutical company develops a new drug, it must test the drug to determine whether or not it is effective. One of the ways that they do this involves deception in the form of a placebo. In such tests, the subjects are divided into two groups. Both groups are told that they are receiving the real drug, but one group is really taking a placebo – a medically neutral product. These tests involve deceiving large numbers of people about the chemicals that they are ingesting, and yet such deception is justified because the drugs that are created with such tests can save millions of lives each year.
   b. We all lie every single day. We tell our friend that she looks great in that new sweater, even if it makes her look terrible. We tell our mother that her pot roast is delicious, even if it is dry and chewy. Each and every day, we lie – not necessarily for any nefarious reasons but for the benefit of others. There is a time and a place for honesty, but there is also a time and a place for deception.

Why? _____
_____
_____

Guidelines for stronger examples:

- As a general rule of thumb, examples which could be proven are stronger than examples which could not be proven. In other words, an example from history – which could be easily verified with a quick Google search – is usually going to be stronger than an example from your personal life, which the reader will just have to take your word on. *Note: This does not mean that your readers will verify your examples – they won't. This simply means that "common" or "public" knowledge will usually carry more weight than your personal knowledge.*
- Because your personal knowledge won't generally carry as much weight, you should limit yourself to no more than one example from your personal experiences.
- When you want to use an example from your personal experiences, you can make the example stronger by telling a little fib: Tell your experience as though it happened to someone else and you read about it somewhere. For example, if your personal experience was that you had trouble with your grades and then you worked really hard to bring them back up, you could write the experience like this: "I recently read a short article about the ways that struggling students improve their grades. Each of the students featured in the article said that no matter how many shortcuts they tried, the only way they were able to improve their grades was through simple hard work." *Don't ever try this on any other writing assignment – on the SAT essay, you know no one will ever check, and to be honest, no one really cares if you fib about your sources; on any other writing assignment, it's outright lying and falsifying sources and that is very BAD.*
- Examples which apply to a broad section of society tend to be more persuasive than examples involving only one person. For example, a survey which polled several thousand people and showed that the vast majority of people find creativity to be more crucial for success than knowledge is more persuasive than the fact that Albert Einstein said that creativity is more important for success than knowledge. Why? Because we tend to be more easily persuaded if lots of people say something than if one person says something, even if that one person is someone well respected. In addition, from a logical standpoint, something that happened to one person – even a famous person – isn't necessarily a rule of thumb, but more likely an exception to the rule. Whereas an example involving lots of people helps to establish the rule of thumb and is therefore somewhat more persuasive.

Practice with Brainstorming Examples

For each of the topics below, reword the question, summarize the excerpt, and brainstorm at least 5 different examples. Then circle the examples you would use in an essay and write out the position your essay would take.

Sample:

> Think carefully about the issue presented in the following excerpt and the assignment below.
>
> If it keeps up, man will atrophy all his limbs but the push-button finger.
> ~Frank Lloyd Wright
>
> **Assignment:** Overall, does technology help or harm society? Plan and write an essay in which you develop your point of view on this issue. Support your arguments with reasoning and examples taken from your reading, studies, experience, or observations.

Reword the Question: *Have modern technologies improved or harmed our society?*

Summarize the Excerpt: *If technology continues to advance, we will lose the ability to perform tasks on our own.*

Possible Examples:

- (*Newspaper article about Facebook: ¾ of people use Facebook at work; college students active on Facebook receive lower grades*)
- *The time my mom's car broke down in the middle of nowhere; cell phone saved her from spending the night in her car*
- (*Newspapers failing because of internet/television; internet/television not as informative so people not well informed*)
- (*The Giver: technology was used to control society; shows dangers of technology*)
- *Instant information because of technology*

Essay Position: *Technology has harmed society.*

1.

> Think carefully about the issue presented in the following excerpt and the assignment below:
>
> > How can one learn to know oneself? Never by introspection, rather by action. Try to do your duty, and you will know right away what you are like.
> >
> > ~Johann Wolfgang von Goethe
>
> **Assignment:** Do you agree that we cannot know who we are and what we are capable of without testing ourselves? Plan and write an essay in which you develop your point of view on this issue. Support your position with reasoning and examples taken from your reading, studies, experience, or observations.

Reword the Question:

Summarize the Excerpt:

Possible Examples:

-
-
-
-
-

Essay Position:

2.
> Think carefully about the issue presented in the following excerpt and the assignment below:
>
> > And in the end, it's not the years in your life that count. It's the life in your years.
> >
> > ~Abraham Lincoln
>
> **Assignment:** Which is more important, to live a long time or to live a full life? Plan and write an essay in which you develop your point of view on this issue. Support your position with reasoning and examples taken from your reading, studies, experience, or observations.

Reword the Question:

_____

_____

Summarize the Excerpt:

_____

_____

_____

Possible Examples:

- _____

- _____

- _____

- _____

- _____

Essay Position:

_____

_____

3.
> Think carefully about the issue presented in the following excerpt and the assignment below:
>
> > You do not lead by hitting people over the head. That's assault, not leadership.
> >
> > ~Dwight D. Eisenhower
>
> **Assignment:** Some leaders prefer to lead by fear and intimidation; others by love and compassion. Do you think it is better for a leader to be loved or feared? Plan and write an essay in which you develop your point of view on this issue. Support your position with reasoning and examples taken from your reading, studies, experience, or observations.

Reword the Question:

_____
_____

Summarize the Excerpt:

_____
_____
_____

Possible Examples:

- _____
- _____
- _____
- _____
- _____

Essay Position:

_____
_____

HOMEWORK

Brainstorming before the Test

This might sound strange, but you can actually begin brainstorming long before you know what essay topic you will write on. This is because most SAT topics tend to fall within certain categories, and so while you cannot predict exactly what you will be asked when you take the SAT, you can safely guess that the essay topic will fall into a certain category.

One of the most difficult things that students face on the SAT is the time limit. 25 minutes is not a lot of time to brainstorm, plan, write, and review an essay. However, if you take the time to create a database of useful and versatile examples long before you take the test, you will make the task much easier. If you already have a bunch of useful examples in mind, brainstorming takes mere moments leaving you plenty of time to craft an excellent essay!

For example, the Civil War could be used to support various positions on various topics. Don't believe us? Look at these samples:

- Many people claim that persistence is the key to success. However, while persistence is certainly helpful, persistence alone is not enough to guarantee that one will be successful. For example, during the Civil War, the Confederate Army fought a losing battle for several years. Although it was clear from very early in the war that the Confederate Army was at a distinct disadvantage and highly unlikely to prevail against the better equipped and better fed United States Army, the Confederate generals pushed on. Their persistence was not met with success; on the contrary, their persistence resulted in a prolonged war that cost lives and money and destroyed land.
- Though our leaders must certainly carry a great deal of responsibility for their decisions because their decisions affect many other people, we as citizens are responsible for our own actions. Our actions cannot be justified by our leaders' decisions. For example, in the Antebellum South, most southern leaders supported the practice of slavery. However, though slavery was a commonly accepted practice and was promoted by southern leaders, individual slave owners were still responsible for violating the basic human rights of their slaves. The fact that the southern leaders supported slavery does not justify the slave owner's actions.
- Society tends to be slow to embrace change. For example, although the institution of slavery was not only morally reprehensible but also economically harmful to the South, southerners were unwilling to eradicate slavery. Even those men who did not own slaves took up arms to defend the practice. It was only after a sound military defeat in a prolonged war that the South gave up slavery, and even then the move was slow and reluctant.

Your Turn to Practice

Look at the following essay topics. Select an example that you could use for all three of the topics. For each topic, write a brief paragraph in which you explain how your example could be used for that topic.

1. Does society tend to embrace change or reject change?

___

2. Do circumstances change the way we perceive things?

3. Does a negative attitude limit our ability to discover new things?

Going Further: SAT Archetypes

This is a list of common themes in SAT essay prompts. You should keep these themes in mind as you continue to compile a list of useful examples.

- **Individuality**
    - *Following the Crowd* (i.e. Is it more valuable for people to fit in than to be unique and different?)
    - *Following Authority* (i.e. Can a group of people function effectively without someone being in charge?)
    - *Following Creativity* (i.e. Is it always better to be original than to imitate or use the ideas of others?)

- **Motivation and Success/Happiness**
    - *Hardship and Success* (i.e. Do people truly benefit from hardship and misfortune?)
    - *Self-Determination and Success* (i.e. Is it more important to do work that one finds fulfilling or work that pays well?)
    - *Ethics and Success* (i.e. Are people's actions motivated primarily by a desire for power over others?)

- **Technological Progress** (i.e. Are there benefits to be gained from avoiding the use of modern technology, even when using it would make life easier?)

- **Heroes** (i.e. Is there a value in celebrating certain individuals as heroes?)

- **Loyalty and Truth** (i.e. Do circumstances determine whether or not we should tell the truth?)

On the next page, you will find a blank chart. You should keep this chart so that you can continue to add new examples to your list. This way, you will be able to create a database of examples that you can use in your essays. This might seem like a lot of work, but it will pay off in the end. **Remember, if you create a database of examples, then when you take the test you won't waste a bunch of time staring at a blank page!**

Unauthorized copying or reuse of any part of this page is illegal.

Version 1.3

Your Example Database

Examples:	Topics Examples Could Relate To:
American Revolution	*Justice, equality, liberty, individuality, heroes, ethics, success/failure*
The Iliad	heroism, leadership, betrayal, loyalty, hubris
Martin Luther	challenge established authority
Civil Rights Movements	
F 451	assimilating into society, losing individualism
Hiroshima bombing	knowledge = burden; "the end justifies the means" - Machiavelli
Batman	vigilante justice, hero w/ questionable values, corrupt society
LOTF	loss of innocence, anarchy + chaos w/o authority
LOTR	loyalty, greed, courage, teamwork, betrayal
Romeo & Juliet	love > death
TKAM	good doesn't always win, racism

Examples:	Topics Examples Could Relate To:

Red Essay 4

Planning the Essay

Although your instincts may tell you to skip the prewriting step of the writing process due to the essay time limit, you should *always* take a minute or two to sketch out a brief outline for your essay. Why? Because by sketching out your essay ahead of time, you will not only be able to write the essay more quickly (you won't have to spend time thinking about what to put in your next paragraph), but you will also be able to write a better organized, clearer, more concise essay.

The Outline

You all know what an outline is. We strongly suggest that you use this knowledge when you write your essays. With a normal writing assignment, we would recommend that you include lots of detail in your outline, because the more details there are in your outline the easier it is to write the essay. However, because you have a fairly short time limit, for the SAT essay we suggest that you only write out a brief and sketchy outline – just enough to remind you of what information you want to include in each paragraph.

You should already have an idea for how to structure an SAT essay: Introduction (including a thesis), a body paragraph for each of your examples (with transitions and topic sentences), and a conclusion that reiterates your position. Knowing your essay format ahead of time makes planning your essay much easier.

Since you already know how you'll structure your essay, you have a blank outline to work with. The outline for any SAT essay will look something like this:

I. Introduction: Position/Thesis
II. Example 1
III. Example 2
IV. Example 3
V. Conclusion: Restate position

The next few pages contain topics for you to practice with. For each topic, reword the question, brainstorm your examples, select your position, and sketch a brief outline.

...fully about the issue presented in the following excerpt and the assignment

...snowflake in an avalanche ever feels responsible.

...oltaire

Assignment: When a large group of people does something wrong, who should be held responsible: the leaders of the group or all members of the group? Plan and write an essay in which you develop your point of view on this issue. Support your position with reasoning and examples taken from your reading, studies, experience, or observations.

Reword the Question:
The weight of a failure should rest not on an entire group of people, but rather, on the leader that led them to failure.

Brainstorm Examples:
- The Illiad: Odysseus led them to danger & peril
- LOTF: Ralph's lack of leadership caused conflict — things went wrong b/c of Jack, his fault
- VBall Coach: Coach can create toxic atmosphere Coach Alex = toxic
- Leader of US in Afghanistan: No organization blamed for deaths

What will your position be?
A leader is responsible for the failure of a group

Use the following page to outline your essay.

...fully about the issue presented in the following excerpt and the assignment

...u can no more win a war than you can win an earthquake.

...eannette Rankin

Assignment: Do you agree that it is impossible to truly win a war? Plan and write an essay in which you develop your point of view on this issue. Support your position with reasoning and examples taken from your reading, studies, experience, or observations.

Reword the Question:

The consequences that result from conflict make it impossible for one side of the war to truly have victory.

Brainstorm Examples:

- Civil War: NO
- Revolutionary War: NO
- 4 French Indian War: NO

What will your position be?

You can win the fighting, but there are always consequences that outweigh the "victory."

Use the following page to outline your essay.

3.
> Think carefully about the issue presented in the following excerpt and the assignment below:
>
> Not everything that is more difficult is more meritorious.
>
> ~Saint Thomas Aquinas
>
> **Assignment:** Is a difficult accomplishment necessarily worthy of honor? Plan and write an essay in which you develop your point of view on this issue. Support your position with reasoning and examples taken from your reading, studies, experience, or observations.

Reword the Question:
_____
_____

Brainstorm Examples:

a. _____
_____

b. _____
_____

c. _____
_____

d. _____
_____

e. _____
_____

What will your position be?
_____
_____

Use the following page to outline your essay.

The Most Important Sentence: The Thesis

that you've learned, at C2 or at school, about writing a strong thesis statement. In
plain what a good thesis statement does.

_____
_____
_____

The thesis statement is perhaps the most important sentence in your entire essay. A big part of your essay score will be based on whether you have a clear thesis statement and whether your thesis statement shows that you have given thought to the topic.

A good thesis statement will:

- Identify the topic
- Give your position on the topic
- Demonstrate a strong analysis of the topic

Most students don't have much trouble with those first two requirements; the problem comes when students attempt to show that they have given thought to the topic. A typical thesis statement will look like this:

Enjoying your work is more important than how much money you earn.

What is the essay topic for this thesis statement? What is the writer's position on the topic?

_____
_____

This thesis statement seems to be a simple rephrasing of the original essay question, doesn't it? When students simply rephrase the original question, we call it a "cookie-cutter" thesis statement because it shows that the student hasn't really given any thought to the topic at hand and is simply borrowing from the essay prompt. What could this writer do to change his thesis statement so that it shows more thought?

_____
_____
_____
_____
_____

Unauthorized copying or reuse of any part of this page is illegal.

Version 1.3

Typical Thesis Statement: Enjoying your work is more important than how much money you earn.

Better Thesis Statement: Finding fulfillment and satisfaction in one's work is far more important than earning a large paycheck.

Excellent Thesis Statement: Although modern society tends to value others based on their net worth, such materialistic value systems fail to recognize the vital importance of job satisfaction and personal fulfillment.

1. What advice would you give to the person who wrote the "typical" thesis statement?

2. What is good about the "better" thesis statement? What advice would you give to the writer to improve upon this thesis statement?

3. What makes the "excellent" thesis statement better than the others?

Although the typical thesis statement does identify the topic and the writer's position, it fails to demonstrate any deeper thought. The second thesis statement goes somewhat further by rephrasing the original question, showing that the writer at least gave some thought to the deeper meaning of the essay prompt. The final thesis statement is by far the strongest because it not only identifies the topic and the writer's position, but also clearly shows that the writer has considered both sides of the issue at hand.

An excellent strategy when writing your thesis statements is to give a nod to the opposing position; this helps to create a more persuasive thesis statement by recognizing that others might not necessarily agree with you, while still maintaining that you have a valid point to make.

> Think carefully about the issue presented in the following excerpt and the assignment below:
>
> > If you cannot work with love but only with distaste, it is better that you should leave your work...and take the alms of those who work with joy.
>
> ~Kahlil Gibran
>
> **Assignment:** Is enjoying your work more important than how much money you earn? Plan and write an essay in which you develop your point of view on this issue. Support your position with reasoning and examples taken from your reading, studies, experience, or observations.

Step One: Reword the original question. The reason that we reword the question while analyzing the essay prompt is not only to help you think about the question more deeply, but also to help you craft a stronger thesis statement. By rephrasing the original question, you can ensure that your thesis statement will not simply take the original question and turn it into a statement.

Is it more important to find fulfilling and satisfying work, or to earn a large paycheck?

Step Two: Define your position on the topic (remember to base your position on the examples you brainstorm!). If we were to stop here and simply turn the reworded question into a statement expressing our position, we would end up with something very similar to the "better" thesis statement on the last page:

Finding fulfillment and satisfaction in one's work is far more important than earning a large paycheck.

Step Three: Since we want a truly excellent thesis statement, we need to go a step further. You should first identify the opposing point of view, and then decide why that view is wrong and your view is right. In this case, the opposing point of view is that it is more important to earn money. There are many ways that we could say that this view is wrong, but one of them is to say that this is a very materialistic point of view that does not recognize other, more important things in life – like having a fulfilling and satisfying job. With this information in hand, we arrive at our "excellent" thesis statement:

Although modern society tends to value others based on their net worth, such materialistic value systems fail to recognize the vital importance of job satisfaction and personal fulfillment.

Time to Practice

Consider the topics that you outlined earlier in this lesson. For each topic, you should have already reworded the question and decided on your position earlier in the lesson. Follow the steps we've discussed to come up with a strong thesis statement for each topic.

1. When a large group of people does something wrong, who should be held responsible: the leaders of the group or all members of the group?

2. Do you agree that it is impossible to truly win a war?

3. Is a difficult accomplishment necessarily worthy of honor?

HOMEWORK

Choose one of the three essay topics you've practiced with today. Use the space below to write an essay for that topic. You will not be timed, but you should try to limit yourself to no more than 17-18 minutes.

Improving Your Examples

Your examples are a big part of your essay. If you include 3 examples, then three out of your five paragraphs will be dedicated solely to your examples and your explanation of your examples.

As we've already discussed, one of the most important things that you will need to do in order to earn a very high essay score is to include *insight* in your essay. We have already discussed a few ways to include insight in your essay, beginning with the way you analyze the prompt. Now we will discuss how to add insight to your explanations and your examples.

Insightful Examples and Explanations

One of the best (and easiest!) ways to demonstrate strong critical thinking skills on the SAT essay is to clearly show that you recognize the complexity of the subject by mentioning both sides of the issue.

Note that this does not mean that you should write an essay that simply compares each side of the issue! The SAT essay is a persuasive essay and you MUST pick a side to argue!

However, as any lawyer, politician, or debater will tell you, you always need to be able to see an issue from all points of view. If you can anticipate the arguments that someone else might make, you can defeat their arguments ahead of time, right?

In an SAT essay, you should do the same thing. If you can think of just one argument that someone could make for the opposite side, then you should mention that potential argument and then explain why it is wrong. This shows your reader that you have considered what others might think, but that you still believe that you are right. *This is evidence of insight.*

For example:

> Topic: Is charity always helpful or can it sometimes become harmful?

> *Many have argued that charity can become harmful if it is allowed to become a crutch, pointing to the adage, "Give a man a fish, feed him for a day; teach a man to fish, feed him for a lifetime." However, this point of view ignores the harsh realities of our society. For instance, at soup kitchens across the country, thousands of those in need receive warm meals each day. Those who would argue that these daily meals provide a crutch and eliminate the motivation to find paying work have never seen the shame and gratitude in the eyes of the needy as they accept a charitable meal; if they could purchase their own food, they would gladly do so to escape the shame of accepting charity. These meals do not provide a crutch to lean on - they are a means of survival. To assume that charity too easily becomes a crutch is to ignore the human dignity of those in need.*

This body paragraph notes an opposing point of view and then uses an example (people at soup kitchens) to disprove it. This demonstrates that the writer has rejected one point of view in favor of another after careful consideration – *insight!*

Obviously, you won't want to do this in ALL of your body paragraphs. It is sufficient to give a brief mention of the opposing point of view – you should spend the bulk of your essay supporting your own opinion rather than defeating the opposing opinion.

Thus, the question becomes: How do you add insight to your other examples?

There are several ways to include insight in your other body paragraphs. First, start with the examples themselves. The more creative and persuasive your examples are, the greater insight you display. You must walk a careful line between coming up with examples quickly and avoiding "obvious" examples.

As a general rule, the first example that pops into your head is probably a fairly obvious one. Odds are good that a lot of other students also thought of that example right away. While you don't want to waste a lot of time trying to think up off the wall examples, you will want to attempt to come up with at least one example that you feel fairly certain no one else will use. When selecting examples, we suggest that you aim for three examples:

- One that is fairly obvious and straightforward (you are limited by time, and straightforward examples are not only easier to come up with but also faster to write about)
- One that is somewhat unique or off the wall
- One that will help to disprove the opposing point of view

Try coming up with three examples that fit these categories for this essay prompt:

> Think carefully about the issue presented in the following excerpt and the assignment below:
>
> > Winning can be just as bad as losing. Confidence can mess you up just as much as fear.   ~Lao Tzu
>
> **Assignment:** Can over-confidence be just as harmful as fear? Plan and write an essay in which you develop your point of view on this issue. Support your position with reasoning and examples taken from your reading, studies, experience, or observations.

1. Simple Example and Brief Explanation:

_____
_____
_____
_____
_____
_____

2. Unique Example and Brief Explanation:

_____
_____
_____
_____
_____
_____

3. Example to Disprove Opposition and Brief Explanation:

_____
_____
_____
_____
_____
_____

Another way to add insight to your essay through your examples is to make sure that your examples are drawn from different sources. If all of your examples are drawn from one source – such as history – your essay becomes just a little bit flatter. The more ground you cover – the more varied your examples are – the more thought you put into your essay.

Beyond the examples themselves, you can add insight to your essay through your explanations. By adding a great deal of details – not only when describing your examples but also when explaining your own logic – you show your reader that you have taken great care to ensure that your writing is clear and easy to understand.

Look at the paragraph below:

> Topic: Creativity is more important than knowledge.
>
> *Without the ability to apply our knowledge in new ways, our society would no longer progress. For instance, without the creativity to use his knowledge in new ways, Thomas Edison would never have been able to invent the light bulb.*

What advice would you give to this paragraph's author?

_____
_____
_____
_____
_____
_____

The original paragraph makes a valid point, but it could be greatly improved. For instance, the author makes the claim that "without the ability to apply our knowledge in new ways, our society would no longer progress." Why would society fail to progress without creativity? What does creativity have to do with progress? Though the author provides the example of Edison using creativity to invent the light bulb, the example alone does not answer these questions. Moreover, the author fails to explain how Edison used creativity to invent the light bulb, making the example itself far less persuasive.

Now look at the second draft of the paragraph:

> *Without the ability to apply our knowledge in new and creative ways, our society would no longer progress. Each and every invention that has ever been created would never have occurred without the ability to utilize existing knowledge in new ways. For example, Thomas Edison's invention of the light bulb was not based merely on his scientific knowledge, but on his ability to apply that knowledge in unique ways. In fact, Edison's final improvement to the light bulb was to add a specific kind of filament, an idea inspired by the material used to make his fishing pole! Regardless of how much factual data Edison might have known, had he lacked the creativity to draw inspiration from such a source, he would not have met with such success.*

What has the author done to improve the paragraph? How is this paragraph more persuasive than the original paragraph?

_____
_____
_____
_____
_____
_____

In the revised paragraph, the author has taken the time to add some useful details. The details he has added answer all of the questions that the original paragraph failed to address. Moreover, these details add to the writer's credibility by demonstrating knowledge on the subject. A credible writer is always more persuasive than a writer who doesn't seem to know much about his subject.

Here are some rules to follow when you write about your examples:

- **Be as specific as possible.** Include as many details as you possibly can. This doesn't mean you need to go home and memorize tons of facts, figures, and dates. If you can't remember exactly when something happened, give a generalized time period (for instance, the Civil War occurred in the mid-1800s), but try to add as many details as you possibly can.
- **Don't make up your own facts.** When you're writing about real facts – things like history, literature, or current events – always assume that your reader will know the facts. If you write about how the Civil War began in 1870, the odds are good that your reader will spot the factual error; you will have just revealed that you have no idea what you're talking about. It is better be vague (i.e. the war occurred in the mid-1800s) than to be wrong. While your graders are not supposed to take your factual accuracy into account when they grade your essays, it is likely that such glaring errors will subconsciously cause the grader to give you a lower score.
- **Explain everything!** You cannot simply assume that your reader will intuitively understand your logic or reasoning. Many students will make a statement of opinion and then offer an example, but they fail to explain exactly how that example supports that opinion. Make sure to clearly and specifically explain each step in your logic!

Time to Practice

Consider the topic below. Pick a position and come up with an example to support your position.

> Think carefully about the issue presented in the following excerpt and the assignment below:
>
> > A man should never be ashamed to own he has been in the wrong, which is but saying...that he is wiser today than he was yesterday.
> >
> > ~Alexander Pope
>
> **Assignment:** Do we learn more from our successes or our failures? Plan and write an essay in which you develop your point of view on this issue. Support your position with specific examples drawn from your studies, reading, experiences, or observations.

Position: _____

_____

Example: _____

_____

In the space below, write a strong persuasive paragraph in which you use your example to support your position.

Go back and reread the paragraph you just wrote. Odds are, no matter how much effort you put into adding insight and detail to your paragraph, you can still add more. In the space below, rewrite your paragraph to make it stronger. If you need some help deciding where to add detail, ask your teacher to read over your original paragraph.

Review What You Learned

In the space below, explain why it is important to include plenty of details in your body paragraphs.

HOMEWORK

Use the following pages to plan and write an essay on the topic below. You will not be timed but you should try to limit yourself to 25 minutes.

> Think carefully about the issue presented in the following excerpt and the assignment below:
>
> Our greatest glory is not in never falling, but in rising every time we fall.
>
> ~Confucius
>
> **Assignment:** Do you agree with the idea that being resilient in the face of failure is essential for success? Plan and write an essay in which you develop your point of view on this issue. Support your position with reasoning and examples taken from your reading, studies, experiences, or observations.

Remember to follow all of the steps that we have covered so far: Reword the question, look at the excerpt, brainstorm your examples, pick your position, outline your essay, write a strong thesis, and write strong body paragraphs!

Red Essay 6

Paragraph Organization

Your overall essay has to show a clear sense of organization, but this requires more than simply remembering to include an introduction and a conclusion. In order to create a well organized essay, each and every paragraph must be well organized.

Parts of a Paragraph

A typical paragraph has three main parts:

- **A topic sentence:** Basically the "thesis statement" of your paragraph. It states the claim that you will prove in your paragraph.
- **A body:** Where you prove the claim you made in your topic sentence.
- **Transitions:** These link each paragraph to the one before/after it. This helps you to create good flow in your essay.

A persuasive paragraph should always *state a claim* and then *support the claim*. For example:

> High schools ought to include mandatory community service projects as a requirement for graduation. In an ideal world, this would not be necessary because students would naturally desire to help their communities; since we do not live in an ideal world, the only way to impart the important life values that community service offers is to require participation in community service projects. Community service projects expand students' horizons by introducing them to people, concepts, and modes of thought that they likely would not otherwise have considered. Studies have shown that this helps students develop better problem solving skills and social skills, and that students who participate in community service projects tend to perform better in school. More importantly, community service teaches students that they have the power to effect change, thereby producing active and engaged citizens. Perhaps if these lessons were more widely preached, if they were mandatory rather than voluntary, then our world would be a more compassionate and caring place.

1. What is the claim stated in this paragraph?

   _____
   _____
   _____

2. How does the author support this claim? What are the arguments he makes? What proof does he offer?

   _____
   _____
   _____
   _____
   _____
   _____

Time to Practice

For each of the topics below, write a brief persuasive paragraph in which you clearly state your claim and then support your claim. Underline your topic sentence (your claim).

1. Should schools and public libraries ban books that do not contain explicit or violent material?

2. Should students be required to learn a second language?

3. Should high schools offer online courses like many colleges do?

4. Should art and/or music classes be mandatory?

Strong Links between Paragraphs

Transitions link your paragraphs together so that one idea flows naturally into the next. There are many, many transitions and transitional phrases that you might use to link your paragraphs, but some are better than others. You should avoid "cookie-cutter" transitions – transitions which are overly simplistic and seem unnatural. Transitions such as "first", "then", "finally", and "in conclusion" often strike the reader as overly obvious. Use of such transitions implies that the transitions were an afterthought – something you included simply because you knew you were supposed to. Just as you need to add insight to the rest of your essay, your transitions should also show a greater degree of thought and skill.

Some ways to add complexity to your transitions:

- **Use less obvious transitions:** Go beyond the basic list of transitions that you probably learned in middle school (first, second, after, next, then, etc.). Add to your repertoire to include higher level transitions and transition phrases such as: Interestingly, significantly, equally important, indeed, in fact, consequently, etc. If you feel like you have difficulty with this, the best way to familiarize yourself with strong writing style skills is to read good writing; you don't have to go find a classic novel – even reading a few news articles from publications such as *The New York Times* or *The Atlantic* each week will help you to become more familiar with good writing skills.
- **Repetition can help transition:** By repeating certain words or phrases, you can help your ideas flow from one paragraph to the next. Look at this example:

    <u>**Modern** society places a great deal of faith in our **ability to multitask**</u>. Although some studies have shown that adding variety to our mental tasks improves our mental agility, societal focus on the skill of multitasking seems to have resulted in collective attention deficit disorder. As a result of our national obsession with constantly performing two or more tasks simultaneously, we seem to have lost the ability to concentrate. National attention is constantly shifting from one topic to another, never staying put long enough to solve important problems or even to see a situation through until the end. Simply look at our news cycle for proof: News corporations are constantly, ceaselessly hunting for the next big story because national focus never stays with one story for more than a day or two.

    <u>This **ability to multitask** has been *further* encouraged by **modern** technology, such as the internet, smart phones, and other mobile devices</u>...

    If you look at the two underlined statements, you can see a certain parallel between them. Both of these paragraphs begin with a transition sentence which contains similar phrasing; despite the similarity, the reader is not left with an annoying sense of repetition but rather with a satisfying flow from one paragraph to the next. The addition of the term "further" in the second paragraph adds to the ease of transition by providing a clear relationship between the first paragraph and the second.
- **Transitions between sentences can also improve flow:** Transitions between paragraphs are vital for your essay's overall organization, but transitions between sentences also help the essay to flow better.
    - <u>Sentences can be linked using pronouns and antecedents</u>: Transitions are all about creating relationships – whether between paragraphs or sentences. By using pronouns that refer to antecedents in another sentence, you create relationships between those sentences. This helps the sentences to flow together. *Be careful to make sure that these*

pronoun/antecedent relationships are clear, though! You don't want to leave your reader guessing about which term your pronoun refers to!
- Repeating words or ideas helps to create relationships between sentences: Just as you can use repetition to link paragraphs, you can also use repetition to link sentences. As always, you want to be careful to avoid being annoyingly repetitive – you should still strive for variety in your word choice and sentence structure – but by repeating a few key phrases or ideas, you can fuse your sentences together better.
- Transitions can also be used for linking sentences: Transitions do not have to be in the first or last sentence of a paragraph, and they are not solely used to link paragraphs together. The ideas within a single paragraph can also be linked through transitions. You should still endeavor to use somewhat higher level transitions such as: in addition, moreover, further, furthermore, similarly, likewise, nevertheless, on the contrary, hence, therefore, accordingly, in sum, etc.
- Parallel sentence structure also aids flow: One way to create a link between two sentences is to use the same or similar sentence structure; this repetition may be less obvious than using the same words or phrases, but it also helps the reader to link the two sentences together. *Again, be careful not be annoyingly repetitive – you still want to include variety, so you should only use repetition when it serves a good purpose!*

Time to Practice

Read the essay below. You will notice that this essay is very choppy – it does not flow well because it lacks transitions. In the space provided, rewrite the essay to include transitions and transition techniques so that the essay flows well.

> *With leadership comes the responsibility to take care of the people under you. A good leader has to consider what is best for everyone he is in charge of. A good leader cannot simply make rash decisions. A good leader must give careful consideration when making choices. Leaders who fail to consider their actions may join the ranks of such poor leaders as King Henry VIII of England and the fictional Galactic President Zaphod Beeblebrox of The Hitchhiker's Guide to the Galaxy.*
>
> *King Henry's first wife failed to give him the son that he needed to ensure that his crown would be safe. King Henry requested permission for a divorce from the Pope. The Pope refused and King Henry decided to separate from the Catholic Church and formed the Church of England. King Henry did not consider how this change might affect the people of England, who had been members of the Catholic Church for centuries. England entered a time of social unrest that ultimately caused many deaths as a result of widespread religious prosecution. King Henry made a rash decision based on selfish impulses and the decision negatively impacted an entire country for decades.*

Zaphod Beeblebrox, President of the Galaxy in Douglas Adams's *Hitchhiker's Guide to the Galaxy*, was known throughout the universe as an absolutely terrible leader. There were many qualities that made Zaphod a poor leader, but one of the most striking was his tendency to make poor decisions without considering their consequences. Zaphod stole the Heart of Gold ship, which not only made him a wanted criminal but also took valuable technology from the hands of the very people he was supposed to represent.

Though leaders often need to make quick decisions in trying circumstances, when time allows, a good leader ought to carefully consider the potential consequences of each decision. Failure to do so may have a terrible impact on the people a leader is supposed to be leading.

Use the space below to rewrite the essay; you should use the techniques discussed in this lesson to improve the essay and to make the ideas flow better.

Organizing Information

In order to craft a well organized essay, each individual paragraph must be well organized. Beyond the basic parts of a paragraph – a topic sentence, a body, and transitions – you must ensure that your paragraph not only fully explains your ideas but that it is also very cohesive and concise. You must undertake a balancing act between providing adequate information without providing too much information, and you must present the information in a logical and easily understood manner.

Look at each of the following paragraphs. All of these paragraphs have been drawn from an essay about the need to take risks in order to succeed, and each paragraph has organization problems. In the space provided, explain what the author has done wrong when organizing each paragraph. The author may have left out important information, presented his information in a confusing manner, or included too much unnecessary information. Offer suggestions for how to improve each paragraph.

1. When Christopher Columbus set sail in 1492, he expected to find a sea route to the Indies. Queen Isabella wanted a good trade route, so she funded his trip. Many of his contemporaries scoffed at this venture, because they did not think that his ideas about the geography of the Earth were correct. Columbus thought that a sea route to Asia would be shorter than travelling over land, but most other people believed that the sea route would be very long - so long that most people thought Columbus would never make it. Columbus ignored such naysayers and risked personal failure, financial and social ruin, and his and his crew's very lives. Ultimately, he failed to discover a new route to the Indies and instead discovered an entirely new continent, permanently altering the course of history. Though, to be fair, Columbus wasn't actually the first European to reach North America - the Norse, led by Lief Erikson, had arrived about 500 years earlier, but the Norse did not really create any lasting settlements. Columbus's discovery, however, had a lasting impact on the Spanish, who soon began colonizing the New World. Had Columbus not taken these risks, our history would be quite different.

_____
_____
_____
_____
_____
_____

2. The Wizard of Menlo Park, Thomas Edison, created over 1,000 inventions. If he had allowed a fear of failure to prevent him from taking chances, many - if not all - of these inventions would never have existed. Instead, Edison persevered; even in the face of failure after failure, Edison continued to alter and test new inventions, ultimately becoming one of the best known inventors in history.

3. "Why did you fail the test?" my mother demanded. "I don't know," my brother sullenly replied. My brother used to have a terrible habit of failing tests, quizzes, or projects. It wasn't that he wasn't smart - he's quite bright - but he never used to put forth any effort in his schoolwork. Now he has overcome his fear of failure and he gets much better grades. I noticed his fear of failure one day when he told me that he didn't want to study because he'd rather do badly and know that it was because he didn't try than fail and know it was because he was too dumb to pass. I immediately realized that my brother's bad grades were not the result of laziness but of fear. Once I began helping him study, his grades improved and he realized that he could get good grades on his own if he put forth the effort. But it took a really long time to get him over his fear of failure. In the end, it was fear that kept my brother from achieving success. If we fear failure, then we can't ever be successful because we won't bother trying to succeed.

HOMEWORK

Plan and write an essay on the topic below. You will not be timed, but you should try to limit yourself to no more than 25 minutes. Be sure to use all of the essay writing steps and information that we have covered so far!

> Think carefully about the issue presented in the following excerpt and the assignment below:
>
> Philosophers are often concerned with how we know things. One position on knowledge posits that in order to appreciate a concept, we must experience its opposite as well. For example, one cannot know what good is until one has encountered evil.
>
> **Assignment:** Do you agree with the claim that one cannot know a concept without knowing its opposite? Plan and write an essay in which you develop your point of view on this issue. Support your position with reasoning and examples taken from your reading, studies, experience, or observations.

Red Essay 7

The Art of Persuasion

All SAT essays are persuasive essays. On any given topic, you will be asked to select a point of view and defend it; you must persuade your reader to agree with you. In this lesson, we will examine different methods for making your writing more persuasive.

Persuasive writers use several different strategies to convince their readers. A writer might appeal to the reader's emotions, logic, or ethics; a writer might use specific evidence to prove a general point; a writer might use statistics, experts, or facts to support an argument. There are any number of ways to persuade people.

As you should already know, one of the best ways to improve your SAT scores – and your reading and writing skills in general – is to read examples of good writing. The same holds true with the art of persuasion; one of the best ways to learn persuasive writing is to read good examples of persuasive writing. As you prepare for the SAT, we strongly suggest that you read editorials and opinion pieces in respected publications such as *The New York Times*.

Consider examples of persuasive writing that you have seen, including advertisements and newspaper editorials. What makes an essay, article, or other writing persuasive?

_____
_____
_____
_____
_____
_____
_____

On the following page, you will find an example of persuasive writing. This example is an essay about Internet censorship. Pay close attention to the persuasive techniques the writer uses and then answer the questions that follow.

Thesis Statement	Each day, millions of people log onto the Internet. Whether for entertainment, work, school, or other purposes, millions of people of all ages and backgrounds utilize the information contained on the worldwide web. Until now, this access has been relatively free of restriction, but this freedom is in danger of becoming yet another government-regulated part of our daily lives. **The Internet's primary value is its role as a world of information which may be freely accessed by all; to erode this freedom would be wrong.**
Counterargument and answer *Logical Appeal* **Factual Support** Ethical Appeal	There are several arguments on either side of the debate about government regulation of the Internet. <u>Many believe that the Internet ought to be censored because it allows underage users open access to undesirable, or even dangerous, material. However, this concern is insufficient reason to limit the freedoms of the millions of Internet surfers.</u> *It is no secret that the Internet contains undesirable material, but whether or not a minor has access to such information can easily be subject to a parent or guardian's control.* **Numerous software programs, such as NetNanny, exist to provide protection against undesirable sites, allowing parents and guardians ample control over what their children are able to see.** There is no need for government intervention when such a simple solution is so readily available. <u>In fact, such unnecessary intervention would only set a dangerous precedent for further government intrusion into the daily lives of citizens, opening the door for invasions of privacy and unfair censorship.</u>
Logical Appeal **Factual Support**	*Not only can people control Internet access at home, but many sites which contain undesirable material are also registering with protection companies to prevent underage web surfers from accessing their content, adding an additional layer of protection between minors and dangerous web content.* **These protection companies provide password protection for sites containing undesirable material. Such programs are becoming more and more widespread; one of the largest site protection companies protects over 11,000 sites. Users register with credit cards and are provided with an account with allows access to protected sites. Since an account requires a credit card, underage access is considerably limited.** This provides a viable alternative to government control of the Internet, an option which restricts underage access to dangerous content but which does so without allowing unfair government intrusion.
Ethical Appeal *Ethical Appeal*	<u>Government intrusion into Internet usage would lead to a myriad of problems, such as how to effectively enforce regulations. Since the government would not be able to charge people for Internet access, how would it enforce regulations without either monitoring the sites that people visit or closing down certain sites altogether?</u> *Either option would result in a "Big Brother" scenario; either average citizens would be spied on, or the First Amendment right to free speech would become a distant memory. The government could not regulate Internet traffic without either invading our privacy or violating the right to free speech.*
Emotional Appeal	**It should anger every American that our government would so publicly try to abridge our freedom. Our rights to free speech and privacy are among the most fundamental ideas that our country is based on. We condemn other countries for oppressing the freedoms of their citizens; we shouldn't allow our government to do the same to us.**

Notice that the writer used several specific techniques:

- A *logical appeal* is an argument that appeals to your reader's reason or common sense. Often, logical arguments simply suggest that common sense shows that the writer is correct. Logical arguments are often supported by facts, expert opinions, or statistics.
- An *emotional appeal* is an argument which appeals to your reader's feelings. Emotional appeals are arguments which attempt to incite anger for the other side, sympathy for the writer's point of view, or other emotional responses to the issue. (On the SAT, examples from your own experiences and observations are often a good source for emotional appeals.)
- An *ethical appeal* is an argument which appeals to a person's sense of fairness or justice. An ethical argument will usually point out that the opposing point of view is somehow unethical or unfair.
- A *counterargument* is something we have already briefly discussed: Offering the argument that your opponent might use and then explaining why that argument is wrong.

Answer the following questions in complete sentences:

1. Which technique did you find most persuasive? Why?

    _____
    _____
    _____
    _____

2. Would the author's "logical appeals" be less persuasive without factual support? Why or why not?

    _____
    _____
    _____
    _____

3. What emotions does the author appeal to? Did you find his emotional appeal effective?

    _____
    _____
    _____
    _____

4. Overall, did you find this essay to be strongly persuasive? Why or why not?

    _____
    _____
    _____
    _____

Time to Practice

Read each of the following statements. For each statement, identify the persuasive technique the writer used. Then, in the space provided, write another one sentence argument, either for or against, using one of the other persuasive techniques. Each statement uses one of the four techniques from the sample essay.

1. Clearly our education system is failing given the recent statistics showing that nearly 1/3 of all graduating seniors have not mastered the basic fundamentals of reading, writing, and math.
   Technique: _____
   Alternative Argument: _____
   _____
   _____

2. The legislation should not pass because adjusting teacher salaries to reflect student test scores would unfairly penalize those teachers who utilize more creative teaching methods and avoid "teaching to the test."
   Technique: _____
   Alternative Argument: _____
   _____
   _____

3. Though many argue that stiffer regulations for the logging industry would harm the economy by eliminating jobs, the truth is that such regulations are necessary in order to prevent the logging industry from destroying entire forests and thereby destroying the industry itself.
   Technique: _____
   Alternative Argument: _____
   _____
   _____

4. Drunk drivers ought to be more harshly punished because their selfish actions too often result in the tragic loss of innocent lives.
   Technique: _____
   Alternative Argument: _____
   _____
   _____

Persuasive Language

Persuasive writers use language in order to help build their cases. By manipulating language in order to make it more persuasive, writers are better able to convince people to agree with them. Some examples of utilizing language to make your writing more persuasive include:

- **Pronoun Usage:** The SAT essay is formal, which means that you may be tempted to shy away from using pronouns such as "you" or "we". However, in some circumstances, the term "we" can actually help to make your writing more persuasive because it brings your reader into your arguments. For instance:

As individuals and as members of a strong society, **we/people** *have a responsibility to care for our/their communities.*

The use of "we" includes both yourself and your reader in the argument, making it more personal. The use of "people" makes the argument impersonal, which also makes it slightly less persuasive.

- **Sensory Language:** Not only does imagery – which is, essentially, using sensory language to create an image in your reader's mind – help to showcase your writing skills, it can also help improve the persuasive aspect of your writing because writing which contains plenty of sensory details is more interesting, and so your reader is more likely to pay attention to your arguments, thus more likely to be persuaded by them.

The once **clear** *lake was now* **brown with trash floating in it***, clearly showing the damaging effects of pollution.* OR
The once **shimmering** *lake was now* **dull with sludge and dotted with discarded cans, bottles and other detritus***, clearly showing the damaging effects of pollution.*

- **Short Sentences:** In an SAT essay, you're primary goal is to show off your writing skills, which means using varied vocabulary and sentence structure. However, while we strongly suggest using a variety of sentence structures and lengths, you can utilize short sentences to emphasize important information. For example:

Despite the vast amounts of research and statistics that underscore the dangers of cigarette smoking, many smokers do not realize the reality of their habit until they have witnessed the final outcome of a lifetime of smoking. **Cigarettes kill.**

- **Emotive Language:** Particularly when using emotional appeals, language which inspires an emotional response tends to be very effective. For example, compare the following sentences:

Animal shelters **euthanize many animals** *each year.* OR
At animal shelters **across the country, thousands** *of* **homeless dogs, cats, puppies, and kittens** *are* **killed** *every year.*

Both sentences make the exact same point, but the second sentence uses emotive language to make the statement more persuasive. By emphasizing how widespread the problem is ("across the country"), how many animals die ("thousands"), what sort of animals (cute little "dogs, cats, puppies, and kittens"), and the true meaning of the sterile term "euthanize" ("killed"), the writer renders his statement much more persuasive. Words have great impact when used correctly.

Time to Practice

For each of the following topics, write a brief persuasive paragraph in which you use at least two of the persuasive language techniques discussed in this lesson.

1. In some countries every young person must serve two years of military service. Should we have a similar policy in the United States?

   What persuasive language techniques did you use?

2. A well-known football coach once said, "Winning isn't everything, it's the only thing." Do you agree or disagree with this statement?

___

What persuasive language techniques did you use?

___

HOMEWORK

Plan and write an essay on the topic below. Be sure to use all of the steps and techniques that we have discussed so far. You will not be timed, but you should try to limit yourself to no more than 25 minutes.

> Think carefully about the issue presented in the following excerpt and the assignment below:
>
> Money is better than poverty, if only for financial reasons.
>
> ~Woody Allen
>
> **Assignment:** Is an individual's financial status the most important factor governing his or her quality of life? Plan and write an essay in which you develop your point of view on this issue. Support your position with reasoning and examples taken from your reading, studies, experience, or observations.

Red Essay 8

Conclusions and Introductions

The first thing that a public speaker learns is that people will generally remember the first and last things that you have said. The same holds true for writing: Your reader will generally remember the first and last things that he has read. This is doubly true for an SAT essay, which your reader will only have about 3 minutes to read. To boost your essay score, you can use this information to your advantage by paying close attention to the quality of your introductions and conclusions.

Framing Your Thesis: Introductions

Your introduction should frame your thesis statement and introduce your position. A strong introduction can accomplish a couple different tasks:

- Logically introducing the topic: Although you are assigned a topic to write about, a good essay will read as though you *decided* to write about this topic.
- Add interest by adding importance: A reader will naturally be more interested and engaged by a topic that seems important. If you add a sense of importance to what you have to say, you will help to add interest to your essay.
- Frame the debate: Your introduction offers you a chance to introduce the topic in a way that is favorable to your stance on the issue.

Look at the sample introductions below:

Introduction 1: *There are those who believe that it is best to live in the moment, appreciating every day as a gift. And there are others who believe that it is far wiser to plan ahead, always preparing for a rainy day. Although we should always strive to appreciate each day, it is best to live with one eye on the future because planning ahead is the only path to security and contentment.*

Introduction 2: *Childhood parables often contain wonderful wisdom which even adults might benefit from. Take, for example, the story of the Grasshopper and the Ant. In this tale, the Grasshopper spends his summer savoring each day, enjoying every moment to the fullest; the Ant, on the other hand, spends the balmy summer days storing food for winter in order to ensure that he will be comfortable during the cold, barren months. When winter arrives, the Grasshopper nearly starves and is forced to appeal to the charity of the better prepared Ant. The moral, of course, is that it is far wiser to look to the future and prepare for a rainy day than it is to blindly live in the moment, a lesson which many modern adults might benefit from.*

The first introduction is adequate – it contains a clear thesis statement and it introduces the topic. But it is flat and boring, uninteresting, doesn't display any real skill with writing, and doesn't particularly help the writer's case. The second introduction, on the other hand, supports the writer's position and adds interest by introducing a well-known story, the moral of which is essentially the writer's thesis.

Why Is the Introduction Important?

Your essay graders will spend no more than three minutes reading your essay, which doesn't leave a lot of time for them to pause and consider and read in any real depth. This time constraint generally means that your grader will likely pay more attention to your first paragraph – your introduction – than to any other paragraph in your essay.

So, what does this mean for you?

In order to help your essay score, you should pay particular attention to your grammar, spelling, language choice, style, and overall writing in your introduction.

Because the essay grader is likely to pay more attention to your introduction than to anything else, you should take great pains to show off your writing abilities in that first paragraph. The introduction is a great place to utilize strong vocabulary, more complex sentences and phrases, and artful writing elements such as metaphors or alliteration. By writing particularly well in your introduction, you will give your grader a better overall impression of your writing abilities.

Strategies for Attention-Grabbing Introductions

The following are strategies for interesting and engaging introductions. Each example deals with the same topic: Technology has harmed society.

Use a personal experience

> *The day my mother made me put down my cell phone was a difficult day indeed. In the few years that I had been on the cellular grid, I had grown immensely attached to the ease of communicating via a few touches of a button. My mother's drastic move was prompted by my tendency to communicate with my own family members via text message...while I was home. Though at first I found my lack of a cell phone to be incredibly inconvenient and difficult to adjust to, I soon realized that my attachment to this little piece of technology had created barriers between myself and those I cared for. Too much a good thing can be dangerous; I fear that our society has indulged in far too much technology, ultimately harming our ability to truly communicate on a personal level.*

How does this introduction help add interest to the essay? How does it help the author make his point?

_____

_____

_____

_____

Use a surprising or shocking fact or statistic

A recent report in the New York Times revealed that the average American teenager sends and receives nearly 80 text messages per day – one text message every 10 minutes for every waking hour. America's youth is clearly addicted to technology, and it is likely that this addiction will have alarming results. Already we see a downward trend in student performance on writing exams, likely due to the 140-chaacter limit on all of those daily text messages. When students have learned to communicate in tiny 140-character sound bites, how can we expect them to communicate effectively as adults? Technology has a time and a place, but is pervasiveness in American society has undoubtedly been harmful.

How does this introduction help add interest to the essay? How does it help the author make his point?

_____
_____
_____
_____

Use a hypothetical situation

Imagine a world in which technology has made life so convenient that we no longer need to leave our homes. Work, education, entertainment, and shopping are available at the touch of a button, rendering the outside world unnecessary. Though such convenience might seem desirable, allowing technology to isolate us from reality carries dangerous consequences, some of which have already begun to appear in our society. Even now we see a decline in student's communication skills and attention spans, and an increasing reliance on modern technology across nearly all demographics. While technology can bring many benefits, among them efficiency and convenience, the overuse of technology has already caused much harm, and unless our reliance on technology is checked it is likely to cause much more dangerous outcomes.

How does this introduction help add interest to the essay? How does it help the author make his point?

_____
_____
_____
_____

Use your own logic and reasoning to explain the topic's importance

We have created a world in which technology is virtually inescapable. From smart phones to GPS systems to laptop computers, technology seems to follow us wherever we go. Yet as invasive as all of this technology sometimes is, we refuse to let it go – we actively choose to be surrounded by the trappings of a technological world. For all of the tasks made faster or easier by technology, those same inventions have created barriers between human beings, isolating each of us in an inescapable technological bubble so that it seems likely that the day will soon come when we devolve into emotionless machines.

How does this introduction help add interest to the essay? How does it help the author make his point?

_____
_____
_____
_____

Time to Practice

For each of the essay questions below, choose a position and write an introduction. Underline the thesis statement in each of your introductions.

1. Is it ever okay to break the law?

   _____
   _____
   _____
   _____
   _____
   _____
   _____

2. Is it necessary to fail in order to gain wisdom?

   _____
   _____
   _____
   _____
   _____
   _____
   _____
   _____

3. Is it more important to achieve personal success or to help others?

4. Is it necessary to take risks in order to succeed?

End With a Bang: Conclusions

If there is one part of the SAT essay that students tend to skip the most, it's the conclusion. Often, this is the result of poor time management: The student did not leave enough time to finish writing the essay and so the conclusion simply isn't there. However, CONCLUSIONS ARE IMPORTANT.

As we discussed earlier in this lesson, readers will usually remember the first and last things they read. If your essay ends abruptly with a body paragraph, your reader will remember your lack of a conclusion which could harm your overall score.

What Should a Conclusion Do?

- **A conclusion should wrap up your essay.** Imagine reading a book and having it just…stop – no resolution, no conclusion, nothing. When you leave off the conclusion of your essay, that's exactly what you're doing. This will make it look like you either ran out of time or you don't know how to write an essay – neither is an impression you want to send to your essay grader.

- **The conclusion should restate your thesis.** Think of this as reminding your essay grader of what your essay is all about. Yes, it's a pretty short essay, and yes, your essay grader should remember what your thesis was – but it's always good to end by reminding your reader of the whole point of your essay. This wraps up the essay in a nice, neat bow so that the same topic and position are clear from beginning to end.

- **Your conclusion should expand your thesis to give it greater purpose.** By expanding your thesis so that it applies to real life, you make your entire essay seem more important, more interesting, more persuasive, and more relevant. Since this is the last thing your essay grader will read before grading the essay, it's good to end on a strong note.

Strategies for Compelling Conclusions

A compelling conclusion will expand your thesis to give it greater purpose, thereby underscoring the importance of what you have to say and adding interest to your overall essay. Some strategies for compelling conclusions include:

- **Challenging the reader:** By issuing a challenge or a call to action to your reader, you involve the reader in your argument and your paper becomes more persuasive. Conclusions that challenge the reader will usually use the pronouns "we" or "our" as a way of bringing the reader into your argument.

  Example:

  Though generation after generation has fought for equality among races, sexes, and classes, inequality still exists in our society. But perhaps if we admit the imperfections of our society, we can begin to address the causes of inequality so that one day we really can be a society of equals.

- **Looking to the future:** Looking to the future can also emphasize the importance of your paper. This strategy is particularly useful when you are discussing a current issue or problem that needs to be solved.

  Example:

  History must remain a cornerstone of any well-rounded education. If we fail to teach our children to learn from the past, if we fail to demonstrate the importance of righting wrongs, if we fail to give future generations the benefit of our wisdom, then we fail ourselves, our ancestors, and all of those who will come after us. We have an obligation to keep history in our classrooms; a failure to do so will only result in further repeats of past mistakes.

- **Posing Questions:** Posing questions, either to your reader or in general, can help readers gain a new perspective on the topic. It may also bring your main ideas together to create a stronger argument.

  Example:

  It is our creativity that drives us to discover new knowledge. Without creativity, our body of knowledge would never expand, we would never discover or create new things, and our society would soon begin to stagnate. How could we ever hope to invent anything without creativity? How could we hope to travel through space, create innovative treatments for illnesses and diseases, or develop new technologies without the spark of inspiration that only creativity can provide?

Time to Practice

For each of the essay topics below you have already written an introduction. Now write conclusions for the same topics.

1. Is it ever okay to break the law?

2. Is it necessary to fail in order to gain wisdom?

3. Is it more important to achieve personal success or to help others?

4. Is it necessary to take risks in order to succeed?

HOMEWORK

Plan and write an essay for the following essay prompt. You will not be timed, but you should try to limit yourself to no more than 25 minutes.

> Think carefully about the issue presented in the following excerpt and the assignment below:
>
> > Education is a kind of continuing dialogue, and a dialogue assumes...different points of view. ~Robert M. Hutchins
> >
> > What does education often do? It makes a straight-cut ditch of a free, meandering brook. ~Henry David Thoreau
>
> **Assignment:** Which of the above statements best represents your beliefs? Plan and write an essay in which you develop your point of view on this issue. Support your position with reasoning and examples taken from your reading, studies, experience, or observations.

Red Essay 9

Adding Flair

The difference between a 5 and a 6 on the SAT essay often comes down to the writer's use of language – his style. An essay which receives a 5 will likely include all of the essential elements of an SAT essay: An introduction, a strong thesis, two or three well explained examples, and a conclusion; it is likely free of most errors and relatively well written, but it also lacks the more advanced vocabulary, variety of language and sentence structure, and artistic flair of a truly strong writer. To earn a 6 on the SAT essay, you must display a strong skill with language, which means developing your essay writing style.

Most people have several different voices. The way that we speak when hanging out with friends is generally different from the way we speak when communicating with teachers or other authority figures. You alter your language based on your audience, and so it is important to consider your audience when writing your essays. Your audience will be your essay graders, and your essay graders are typically high school or college English teachers; they have high standards, and you should always try to meet them.

Look at these examples to see how your writing style can make a difference to the overall impression of your essay. Each example discusses the idea that fear can be beneficial.

Style Sample 1:

Since the creation of society, governments have used fear as a tool for civilization. By creating harsh punishments for criminals, governments are better able to reduce crime, a practice which has been in use for many centuries. While modern punishments are certainly lax by historical standards, even today's governments utilize societal fear of recrimination to discourage crime. By setting long jail terms for drug-related crimes or the death penalty for certain crimes, the government instills in the citizens a fear of facing punishment for lawbreaking. While this fear certainly doesn't prevent all crimes, it unquestionably prevents the vast majority of citizens from breaking the law. Thus, fear can be a beneficial tool to ensure an upstanding citizenry.

Style Sample 2:

Our government uses fear to get people to follow laws. They make stiff punishments for people who break laws, like the death penalty for murderers or long jail terms for drug dealers. These punishments make people afraid to break the laws because they are afraid of being executed or put in jail. If people were not afraid of being punished, they would be more likely to break the law. Fear stops people from breaking the law, so fear can sometimes be beneficial.

Both of these paragraphs discuss the same example and make the same argument, but one of these paragraphs is clearly better than the other. Which paragraph do you think is more impressive? What specific things did the author do to make this paragraph more impressive?

_____
_____
_____

There are several things that you can do to improve your writing style. Some suggestions include:

- **Trim sentences:** Cut some of your longer or more confusing sentences down to make your language more concise. For example:

  Many people struggle with the decision of whether to find work that pays well and provides a good living or to find work that may not pay well but that is fulfilling. *BECOMES*

  Many people struggle with the decision of whether to seek work that pays well or work that is fulfilling.

- **Combine sentences:** While you should always strive for concise writing, you also need to make sure that you include variety in your sentence structure. Essays which contain a long series of sentences with very similar sentence structure can seem overly simple or even childish; combining some shorter sentences can help to add sophistication to your writing. For example:

  He was a partner in a big law firm. He was really good at his job. He made lots of money. *BECOMES*

  He was a partner in a large law firm, a very talented attorney who earned a large salary.

- **Avoid repetitive language:** Always try to keep both your word choice and your sentence structures from being too predictable and repetitive. Not only does this make your writing seem less sophisticated, it also makes it boring and demonstrates a poor grasp of language. The example above demonstrates this. In the example above, you can see that both the word choice (particularly the overuse of "he") and the sentence structure were repetitive, but that the rewritten sentence is less repetitive and therefore more sophisticated.

- **Add vivid and sophisticated vocabulary:** The SAT essay is the perfect place to use those more sophisticated SAT words that you've been studying. You might also consider using more formal transitions such as "thus" or "therefore" – the types of words which you almost never use in daily conversation, but that you might see in a highly regarded newspaper. Even small changes – "father" instead of "dad", or "large" instead of "big" – can help to improve the overall tone of your writing by adding sophistication and polish.

  For a long time my dad thought about quitting his job because it stressed him out so much. *BECOMES*

  For many years my father struggled with the decision to leave his job because his position caused him a great deal of stress.

Being Concise

It is important that you be concise on the SAT essay; long, rambling sentences are likely to confuse your reader. Rewrite each of the sentences below to make them more concise. You may shorten the existing sentence, break it into multiple sentences, or use any other method you feel comfortable with.

1. If everyone followed the crowd then society wouldn't grow and progress because no one would ever think up new and different ideas because they would all be following the ideas that everyone else already follows and so nothing would ever improve.

2. We have a responsibility to help those less fortunate than ourselves, not only because compassion demands such actions but also because we live in a global and interconnected society in which the wellbeing of one person is directly related to the wellbeing of everyone else so if we help out those who are in need eventually everyone will be better off.

3. Modern society has become quite greedy, something which can be clearly seen during the holiday season which has become a retailer's dream instead of the warm and loving time of togetherness that it once was, a time for buying and receiving presents rather than showing goodwill and charity to others.

4. The human mind is programmed to remember bad times more easily than good times, which explains why human beings tend to learn far more from making mistakes than from doing things right because we remember when we mess up more easily than we remember when we succeed.

Combining Sentences

Many students write essays that contain a lot of short, simple sentences. Such essays quickly become unsophisticated, repetitious, and boring. It is important to include varied sentence structures in order to add interest and sophistication to your writing. Read the following paragraph. Then, in the space provided, rewrite the paragraph to include more varied sentence structure.

It is more important to plan for the future than to live for the moment. We should appreciate our time on Earth. But our lives would not be very good if we only lived for the moment and didn't plan for the future. By not planning for the future we cause ourselves unhappiness. For example, my sister was very excited when she got into her top choice college. She insisted on going no matter what. She went to her dream school even though she didn't know how she would pay for it. By not planning for the future, she put herself into lots of debt. Years later she is still making huge loan payments. If she had planned better, her life would be easier. If people don't plan for the future, then they won't be able to live for the moment.

Avoiding Repetition

Because of the limited time period, students are often in such a rush that they don't even notice when they use the same word or phrase multiple times throughout the essay. A very repetitious essay may seem childish or poorly written, even if it is technically grammatically correct. As a general rule of thumb, you should avoid using the same word or phrase more than twice in the same paragraph. Read the following paragraph. Then, in the space provided, rewrite the paragraph to eliminate repetitious language.

Many people struggle with the decision of whether to find work that pays well and provides a good living or to find work that may not pay well but that is fulfilling. My dad is a perfect example. He was a partner in a big law firm. He was really good at his job. He made lots of money. But he also worked really long hours and he was always too tired. He was very unhappy. He wanted to quit and become a teacher. He worried that our family would be hurt if he didn't make as much money. He stayed at his job for a long time. He thought he needed to make a lot of money. After a long time, he decided to go back to school to be a teacher. Now we have a smaller house. Our cars cost less money. But we also have my dad with us more often. And he is much happier. Even though we have less money, we learned that there are more important things than money. Money doesn't buy happiness.

Adding Sophistication through Word Choice

Your choice of words can have a huge impact on the overall impression of your essay. One of the best ways to impress your essay grader is to include a variety of vivid, sophisticated vocabulary words – *just make sure you're using those words correctly!* You should also make sure that each high level word that you use – those tough SAT vocabulary words such as dichotomy, entropy, quizzical, malodorous, or beneficent – has an actual purpose in your essay. Don't fill your entire essay with words that you aren't really comfortable using – your discomfort will show in your writing and your essay will seem pompous and fake.

Think of $5 words as a spice – too much and your essay is too spicy to be edible, too little and it is bland.

You don't have to use fifty really difficult vocabulary words to give your essay polish – simply replacing common words with slightly more sophisticated words can make a huge impact.

For example:

> There were lots of ducks in the pond.
>
> *A **large group** of ducks **floated** in the pond.*
>
> The trip was pretty even though it took forever.
>
> *The trip was **truly lovely despite its length.***
>
> Even though the train's nonstop whistling was very loud, I fell asleep right away.
>
> ***Although** the train's **incessant** whistling was **quite** loud, I fell asleep **instantly.***

In each example, you can see how changing or adding a word here and there can instantly make a sentences seem more polished. Some suggestions for adding polish to your writing:

- Try to avoid referencing yourself unless you are speaking about a first-hand experience. In other words, avoid phrases such as "I think," "I believe," or "in my opinion." Instead of writing "I think that people should spay and neuter their pets," leave off the "I think" and simply say, "People should spay and neuter their pets."
- Avoid writing in the same way that you speak. When you speak, you don't have the luxury of selecting your words carefully, and so your word choice will almost always be less sophisticated when you speak than it should be when you write. Some examples of using more sophisticated terms in writing include:
    - Very → Quite, extremely, exceedingly, incredibly
    - Really → Actually, in fact, in truth, truthfully
    - Even though → Despite, although, in spite of
    - Lots of/A lot → many, several, numerous, countless, various
- Don't use contractions in formal writing. Write the contraction out instead.
- Use vivid nouns and verbs. For instance, in the first example above, the author rewrote the sentence to use the active verb "floated" rather than the passive "were in". Active verbs tend to be more vivid and vivid verbs make your writing more interesting.
- Think like a thesaurus. The secret to good writing is to have an expansive vocabulary – this is true not only for the SAT essay but also for anything and everything you will ever write in life. Make it a daily habit to come up with alternative words for terms you use throughout the day. In other

words, when you come across a commonly used word in your reading, immediately try to come up with three or four alternative words or phrases that could be used in its place. This is will train your mind to quickly think of alternative phrasing, which will better enable you to come up with more sophisticated terminology when you write.

- When you read through your essay before your time is up, keep your eyes peeled for any terms that strike you as somewhat simple, unsophisticated, or even childish. If you spot a word or phrase that you know could be more sophisticated, fix it!

Rewrite each of the following sentences to add sophistication.

1. There are lots of times where people follow the crowd instead of making their own decisions but this kind of thinking is bad for society.

2. A lot of leaders make snap decisions without thinking about them enough but they really should think about all of their decisions carefully because lots of those decisions affect lots of people.

3. Things that are easily achieved aren't really worth having because we don't really value things that were just handed to us and that we didn't really work for.

4. People tend to ignore good advice because we learn better from mistakes than things people say to us.

5. Sometimes difficulties are really blessings in disguise only we don't realize it until later when we look back.

HOMEWORK

Plan and write an essay based on the essay prompt below. You will not be timed, but you should try to limit yourself to no more than 25 minutes.

> Think carefully about the issue presented in the following excerpts and the assignment below:
>
> Prudence shall be our guiding principle. When faced with a conflict, or a divergent path in the course of life, we shall always make caution our ally. Recklessness and rash action lead not to fruitfulness, but only to regret at the haste of our decisions.
>
> Oftentimes, people ask me how I have been so successful in business…When I reflect on my decisions, I realize that the key to my success is nothing more than simple opportunism. When I saw an opening, I jumped at it. While everyone else was standing still, agonizing over the correct course of action, I went in feet first, with no hesitation. That is the key to my success.
>
> **Assignment:** Consider the two contrasting statements above. Which best reflects your view on life? Plan and write an essay in which you develop your point of view on this issue. Support your position with reasoning and examples taken from your reading, studies, experience, or observations.

Editing

Think back to the first lesson in this belt in which we discussed the importance of time management. In that lesson, we suggested that you save the last couple of minutes to read through your essay and correct any errors or awkward wording. We've already discussed ways to improve your style; in this lesson, we will discuss the importance of editing for grammar and spelling.

Why lose points simply because you didn't take one or two minutes to reread your essay and fix your mistakes? You'd be amazed how often students make simple, cosmetic grammar or spelling errors that could easily have been avoided just by reading over the essay before the time was up. This sends a poor message to your reader and is likely to cost you on your final essay score.

Why Bother?

Many students believe that the time limit on the SAT essay eliminates the need for editing. Why bother editing when your essay grader understands that you were operating on a shortened time frame? The truth is that you are writing for an audience made up of current or former English teachers – people who have been well trained to pay close attention to language usage, spelling, and grammar. If your audience will pay attention to such things, so should you.

The SAT essay is a persuasive essay. If we consider other forms of persuasive writing, we can see how numerous spelling or grammar errors might harm the credibility of the author, thus making the writing less persuasive. After all, how can you take the word of someone who fails to communicate his ideas properly?

Consider it in this light: How would you react if you opened a newspaper and read an editorial filled with grammar and spelling errors? How would this affect your opinion of the writer and his opinions?

Common Errors in a Timed Essay

Aside from spelling errors, these are the errors that our essay graders have listed as the most common problems in our students' essays. Here's what our essay graders have to say about them:

A/an: You all know the rules about a and an – a before a consonant (a tree) and an before a vowel (an apple) – yet we see these errors again and again. This is a mistake that can and should be fixed before your time is up.
   Example: In the story, the boy bought a bean which grew into an huge stalk.

Affect/Effect: Almost all students have problems with affect and effect. It might help you to pronounce the words differently in your own mind, because though these words are similar, *they are not the same*. Affect is a verb that means "to change something". Effect is usually a noun that means "a change" or "a result". When you **affect** something, you have an **effect** on it.
   Example: We can all effect our communities.

Its/It's: This is another very common usage error. Always remember that "its" means "it possesses something" and that "it's" means "it is".
   Example: Congress sets it's own salary.

There/Their/They're: Your school teachers have probably been nagging you about this little usage rule since the 2nd grade. They're right, though – lots of students have trouble with the proper usage of there, their, and they're. As a refresher: There has to do with location (i.e. "It is over there") or it can be used as a pronoun (i.e. "There is a stain"); Their involves multiple people possessing something (i.e. "It's their dog"); and They're is a contraction meaning "they are" (i.e. "They're going to the circus").
   Example: They fought for there rights.

Then/Than: "Than" has nothing to do with time; it is a comparative word. "Then" involves time order. You can be bigger **than** something, but you cannot be bigger *then* something. You can be small and **then** grow large, but you cannot be small and *than* grow large.
   Example: Than the government passed a law about homelessness.

Subject/Verb Agreement: Always check to make sure that your subjects and your verbs agree. You should always look to see that singular subjects have singular verbs, and that plural subjects have plural verbs.
   Example: Millions of people has suffered because of this.

Verb Tense Agreement: It's very common for students to begin writing in one tense, and end up writing in a completely different tense. If you start out in the past tense, don't suddenly start writing in the present tense. Not only does it confuse your reader, it also harms the overall impression of your writing skills.
   Example: In the book, Huck tells many lies but Huck still has principles – for example, he refused to help the Duke and Dauphin steal from the Wilks sisters even though they threaten him.

Comma Abuse: A lot of students either pepper commas throughout their essay so that nearly every sentence has a comma (whether it needs it or not), or they forget to use commas altogether. There are a lot of rules about comma use, but when you write the essay you should follow this general rule of thumb: Read the sentence in your head; if there is a natural pause, you probably need a comma.

Unauthorized copying or reuse of any part of this page is illegal.

Version 1.3

Time to Practice

Take a few minutes to look at the essay below. The essay contains a lot of common errors and spelling errors. Revise and edit the essay to improve its grammar and spelling score.

The recipe for success changes depending on whom one ask. Some might say that luck is the key ingredient others might claim intellegence or creativity to be vital. While such ingredients are surely important the one trait necessary for success of any kind is dogged persistence.

I first learned this lesson, when I began high school. Always before, I had been able to achieve remarkably high grades, with remarkably little effort. Despite taking the most rigorus classes available I rarely studied and yet I still earned top grades. I had not expect this trend to change significntly upon entering high school and I could not have been more incorrect. After just one week in high school my grades had plumeted. My parents' concern was nothing compared to my personal disappointment and I resolved to improve. My first plan, was an utter failure, that revolved around a four leaf clover; I clearly lacked the luck of the Irish. My next plan is to cram for my exams; I studied intensely for long bouts the night before my tests. Though this was more work than I had ever put forth before, it still had little affect. Finally, I had no choice but to resort to prolonged and regular study schedules. Gradually, my grades improved, and I realized that no amount of intelligence, or luck can replace the benefits of dedication, and persistence.

I am certainly not the first person to recognize this valueable lesson. Well over an century ago, Thomas Edison faced similar struggles while attempting to invent a lasting electric light bulb. In fact a reporter once asked him how it felt to have failed 700 times? Edison replied that he did not failed once; he had merely proved 700 ways to make a light bulb that will not work. Edison continued to labor over his invention ultimately creating the first practical electric light bulb after thousands of failed attempts. Edison widely recognized as a genius certainly did not lack intelligence or creativity. Yet no amount of intelligence or creativity could help Edison without his stuborn persistence. It was only because Edison refused to give up that he have entered public consciousness as one of the greatest inventors of all time.

Edison is one of many in a long line of Americans whose successes relies primarily on a determination to succeed. In fact, this country likely would not exist – and certainly not in it's current form – if not for the persistence of our forbarers: First the colonists who doggedly clung to a rough and uncivilized land facing starvation violence and untold difficulties for the chance at a new life; then the Patriots who fought an uphill battle for freedom ignoring failure after failure and ultimately winning the day; next the

49ers who faced the unknown crossing thousands of miles of completely uncivilized land for the merest hope of success. Later after the states were all in place and the country was fully discovered women marched to earn the right to vote waging a decades-long fight for equality. Still later African-American men and women stages rallies and marches gave stirring speeches and waged legal battles to win success for the Civil rights Movement. Our country had been a success because we are a stubborn and determined people undaunted by failure or difficulty.

Luck is wonderful but fickle. Intelligence and creativity are amazing asets to possess, but are worthless without the determination to succeed. Only through persistance can we be assured of success because he who refuses to give up is most likely to prevail.

Aside from the grammar and spelling errors, what did you think of this essay? What did the author do right? What did he do wrong? How did the grammar and spelling errors affect your opinion of the essay?

_____
_____
_____
_____
_____
_____
_____
_____
_____
_____
_____
_____
_____
_____
_____
_____

Putting It All Together

Now that we have discussed how to edit and revise your essays – adding style and polish, correcting any errors, and ensuring that the essay is well written – it's time to put your knowledge to use. Find an essay you wrote for homework in one of the other lessons. Then edit and revise the essay to ensure that it is well written.

HOMEWORK

They say that the best way to learn something is to teach it to someone else. Use the pages provided to write a letter to friend or a family member explaining how to get a perfect score on the SAT essay. Imagine that the person you are writing to has little or no knowledge about the SAT essay section and write a very detailed explanation!

Red Essay 11

Practice Essay

Plan and write an essay on the topic below. You will not be timed, but you should try to limit yourself to no more than 25 minutes. When you're finished with your essay, use the rubric to evaluate your essay.

> Think carefully about the issue presented in the following excerpt and the assignment below:
>
> What is the price of liberty? This question is often asked in civics and political science classes across the country. Is liberty a natural human right, or must it be earned, won or purchased? An examination of history leads one to conclude that liberty is not a natural right – slavery, tyranny, and oppression are as old as humanity. So at what cost does liberty come? For many of history's great liberators, the answer to this question is clear. The cost of liberty should be no less than the ultimate cost – one's life.
>
> **Assignment:** Do you agree that freedom is not a natural right, but something which must be earned, won or purchased? Plan and write an essay in which you develop your point of view on this issue. Support your position with reasoning and examples taken from your reading, studies, experience, or observations.

Essay Scoring Rubric

Instructions for use: This rubric is based on the rubric used by College Board SAT Essay Graders. For each category, assign the essay a score between 1 and 6. The overall essay score should be the average of the scores from each category. For example, if an essay scores a 4 in three categories and a 3 in two categories, the overall score is a 4. Always round to the nearest whole number. Use this rubric to score your essay. Be honest with yourself! The more critical you are, the more you can improve!

Score	Response and Support	Organization	Language Choice	Sentence Structure	Grammar, Usage, & Mechanics
6	Insightful response with specific, concrete, and clearly relevant examples cited as support.	Clearly focused, smooth progression of ideas.	Varied, high level, and accurate vocabulary.	Substantial variety, few if any mistakes.	Very few and insignificant errors, if any.
5	Effective response, with fairly specific and generally relevant examples cited as support.	Focused, smooth progression of ideas.	Appropriate vocabulary.	Frequent variety, few mistakes.	More or less free of errors, errors do not interfere with meaning.
4	Response is there, but the examples aren't very specific or are entirely hypothetical and their relevance is barely adequate.	Generally focused, ideas progress but not very smoothly.	Adequate but inconsistent use of vocabulary.	Some variety, some mistakes.	Some errors.
3	Response is there, but the examples don't cut it.	Limited focus, ideas don't progress from one to another.	Weak vocabulary or occasionally poor word choice.	No variety, some mistakes.	A variety of errors.
2	Response is vague, and the examples are inappropriate or insufficient.	Poor focus, problems with progression of ideas.	Very limited vocabulary or frequently poor word choice.	No variety, persistent mistakes.	Enough errors to create confusion.
1	No response, no examples.	Unfocused, confusing progression of ideas.	Basic errors in vocabulary.	No variety, serious flaws.	Persistent errors that consistently obscure the meaning.

In your opinion, what is the weakest aspect of this essay? What can you do to improve?

___

What is the strongest aspect of this essay? How would you advise others to do as well?

___

Practice Essay

Plan and write an essay on the topic below. You will not be timed, but you should try to limit yourself to no more than 25 minutes. When you're finished with your essay, use the rubric to evaluate your essay.

> Think carefully about the issue presented in the following excerpt and the assignment below:
>
> One revolutionary outcome of the capitalistic system is the overwhelming importance placed on the concept of "ownership." In fact, many non-capitalistic systems have no equivalent concept, with the members of the society sharing essential material goods and having no need to claim ownership over any piece of land or space. The emphasis on ownership has led to a hyper-developed sense of private property, which can manifest itself in extremely selfish behavior, such as the hoarding of goods, that apparently runs counter to biological needs for cooperation among humans.
>
> **Assignment:** Do you agree that the concept of "ownership" can be negative? Plan and write an essay in which you develop your point of view on this issue. Support your position with reasoning and examples taken from your reading, studies, experience, or observations.

Essay Scoring Rubric

Instructions for use: This rubric is based on the rubric used by College Board SAT Essay Graders. For each category, assign the essay a score between 1 and 6. The overall essay score should be the average of the scores from each category. For example, if an essay scores a 4 in three categories and a 3 in two categories, the overall score is a 4. Always round to the nearest whole number. Use this rubric to score your essay. Be honest with yourself! The more critical you are, the more you can improve!

Score	Response and Support	Organization	Language Choice	Sentence Structure	Grammar, Usage, & Mechanics
6	Insightful response with specific, concrete, and clearly relevant examples cited as support.	Clearly focused, smooth progression of ideas.	Varied, high level, and accurate vocabulary.	Substantial variety, few if any mistakes.	Very few and insignificant errors, if any.
5	Effective response, with fairly specific and generally relevant examples cited as support.	Focused, smooth progression of ideas.	Appropriate vocabulary.	Frequent variety, few mistakes.	More or less free of errors, errors do not interfere with meaning.
4	Response is there, but the examples aren't very specific or are entirely hypothetical and their relevance is barely adequate.	Generally focused, ideas progress but not very smoothly.	Adequate but inconsistent use of vocabulary.	Some variety, some mistakes.	Some errors.
3	Response is there, but the examples don't cut it.	Limited focus, ideas don't progress from one to another.	Weak vocabulary or occasionally poor word choice.	No variety, some mistakes.	A variety of errors.
2	Response is vague, and the examples are inappropriate or insufficient.	Poor focus, problems with progression of ideas.	Very limited vocabulary or frequently poor word choice.	No variety, persistent mistakes.	Enough errors to create confusion.
1	No response, no examples.	Unfocused, confusing progression of ideas.	Basic errors in vocabulary.	No variety, serious flaws.	Persistent errors that consistently obscure the meaning.

Version 1.3   Unauthorized copying or reuse of any part of this page is illegal.

In your opinion, what is the weakest aspect of this essay? What can you do to improve?

_____
_____
_____
_____
_____
_____
_____
_____
_____
_____

What is the strongest aspect of this essay? How would you advise others to do as well?

_____
_____
_____
_____
_____
_____
_____
_____
_____
_____

Red Essay 13

Practice Essay

Plan and write an essay on the topic below. You will not be timed, but you should try to limit yourself to no more than 25 minutes. When you're finished with your essay, use the rubric to evaluate your essay.

> Think carefully about the issue presented in the following excerpts and the assignment below:
>
> College isn't the place to go for ideas.
> ~Helen Keller
>
> Next in importance to freedom and justice is popular education, without which neither freedom nor justice can be permanently maintained.
> ~James A. Garfield
>
> **Assignment:** Does higher education stifle ideas and freedom, or is it essential to them? Plan and write an essay in which you develop your point of view on this issue. Support your position with reasoning and examples taken from your reading, studies, experience, or observations.

Essay Scoring Rubric

Instructions for use: This rubric is based on the rubric used by College Board SAT Essay Graders. For each category, assign the essay a score between 1 and 6. The overall essay score should be the average of the scores from each category. For example, if an essay scores a 4 in three categories and a 3 in two categories, the overall score is a 4. Always round to the nearest whole number. Use this rubric to score your essay. Be honest with yourself! The more critical you are, the more you can improve!

Score	Response and Support	Organization	Language Choice	Sentence Structure	Grammar, Usage, & Mechanics
6	Insightful response with specific, concrete, and clearly relevant examples cited as support.	Clearly focused, smooth progression of ideas.	Varied, high level, and accurate vocabulary.	Substantial variety, few if any mistakes.	Very few and insignificant errors, if any.
5	Effective response, with fairly specific and generally relevant examples cited as support.	Focused, smooth progression of ideas.	Appropriate vocabulary.	Frequent variety, few mistakes.	More or less free of errors, errors do not interfere with meaning.
4	Response is there, but the examples aren't very specific or are entirely hypothetical and their relevance is barely adequate.	Generally focused, ideas progress but not very smoothly.	Adequate but inconsistent use of vocabulary.	Some variety, some mistakes.	Some errors.
3	Response is there, but the examples don't cut it.	Limited focus, ideas don't progress from one to another.	Weak vocabulary or occasionally poor word choice.	No variety, some mistakes.	A variety of errors.
2	Response is vague, and the examples are inappropriate or insufficient.	Poor focus, problems with progression of ideas.	Very limited vocabulary or frequently poor word choice.	No variety, persistent mistakes.	Enough errors to create confusion.
1	No response, no examples.	Unfocused, confusing progression of ideas.	Basic errors in vocabulary.	No variety, serious flaws.	Persistent errors that consistently obscure the meaning.

Unauthorized copying or reuse of any part of this page is illegal.

Version 1.3

In your opinion, what is the weakest aspect of this essay? What can you do to improve?

What is the strongest aspect of this essay? How would you advise others to do as well?

Practice Essay

Plan and write an essay on the topic below. You will not be timed, but you should try to limit yourself to no more than 25 minutes. When you're finished with your essay, use the rubric to evaluate your essay.

> Think carefully about the issue presented in the following excerpts and the assignment below:
>
> I never saw an ugly thing in my life: for let the form of an object be what it may – light, shade and perspective will always make it beautiful.
> ~John Constable
>
> If there is one thing worse than being an ugly duckling in a house of swans, it's having the swans pretend there's no difference.
> ~Teena Booth
>
> **Assignment:** Is it true that there are no truly ugly things? Plan and write an essay in which you develop your point of view on this issue. Support your position with reasoning and examples taken from your reading, studies, experience, or observations.

Essay Scoring Rubric

Instructions for use: This rubric is based on the rubric used by College Board SAT Essay Graders. For each category, assign the essay a score between 1 and 6. The overall essay score should be the average of the scores from each category. For example, if an essay scores a 4 in three categories and a 3 in two categories, the overall score is a 4. Always round to the nearest whole number. Use this rubric to score your essay. Be honest with yourself! The more critical you are, the more you can improve!

Score	Response and Support	Organization	Language Choice	Sentence Structure	Grammar, Usage, & Mechanics
6	Insightful response with specific, concrete, and clearly relevant examples cited as support.	Clearly focused, smooth progression of ideas.	Varied, high level, and accurate vocabulary.	Substantial variety, few if any mistakes.	Very few and insignificant errors, if any.
5	Effective response, with fairly specific and generally relevant examples cited as support.	Focused, smooth progression of ideas.	Appropriate vocabulary.	Frequent variety, few mistakes.	More or less free of errors, errors do not interfere with meaning.
4	Response is there, but the examples aren't very specific or are entirely hypothetical and their relevance is barely adequate.	Generally focused, ideas progress but not very smoothly.	Adequate but inconsistent use of vocabulary.	Some variety, some mistakes.	Some errors.
3	Response is there, but the examples don't cut it.	Limited focus, ideas don't progress from one to another.	Weak vocabulary or occasionally poor word choice.	No variety, some mistakes.	A variety of errors.
2	Response is vague, and the examples are inappropriate or insufficient.	Poor focus, problems with progression of ideas.	Very limited vocabulary or frequently poor word choice.	No variety, persistent mistakes.	Enough errors to create confusion.
1	No response, no examples.	Unfocused, confusing progression of ideas.	Basic errors in vocabulary.	No variety, serious flaws.	Persistent errors that consistently obscure the meaning.

Version 1.3   Unauthorized copying or reuse of any part of this page is illegal.

In your opinion, what is the weakest aspect of this essay? What can you do to improve?

What is the strongest aspect of this essay? How would you advise others to do as well?

Red Essay 15

Practice Essay

Plan and write an essay on the topic below. You will not be timed, but you should try to limit yourself to no more than 25 minutes. When you're finished with your essay, use the rubric to evaluate your essay.

> Think carefully about the issue presented in the following excerpt and the assignment below:
>
> In crisis is cleverness born.
> ~Chinese Proverb
>
> **Assignment:** Can crises benefit us by fostering creativity? Plan and write an essay in which you develop your point of view on this issue. Support your position with reasoning and examples taken from your reading, studies, experience, or observations.

Essay Scoring Rubric

Instructions for use: This rubric is based on the rubric used by College Board SAT Essay Graders. For each category, assign the essay a score between 1 and 6. The overall essay score should be the average of the scores from each category. For example, if an essay scores a 4 in three categories and a 3 in two categories, the overall score is a 4. Always round to the nearest whole number. Use this rubric to score your essay. Be honest with yourself! The more critical you are, the more you can improve!

Score	Response and Support	Organization	Language Choice	Sentence Structure	Grammar, Usage, & Mechanics
6	Insightful response with specific, concrete, and clearly relevant examples cited as support.	Clearly focused, smooth progression of ideas.	Varied, high level, and accurate vocabulary.	Substantial variety, few if any mistakes.	Very few and insignificant errors, if any.
5	Effective response, with fairly specific and generally relevant examples cited as support.	Focused, smooth progression of ideas.	Appropriate vocabulary.	Frequent variety, few mistakes.	More or less free of errors, errors do not interfere with meaning.
4	Response is there, but the examples aren't very specific or are entirely hypothetical and their relevance is barely adequate.	Generally focused, ideas progress but not very smoothly.	Adequate but inconsistent use of vocabulary.	Some variety, some mistakes.	Some errors.
3	Response is there, but the examples don't cut it.	Limited focus, ideas don't progress from one to another.	Weak vocabulary or occasionally poor word choice.	No variety, some mistakes.	A variety of errors.
2	Response is vague, and the examples are inappropriate or insufficient.	Poor focus, problems with progression of ideas.	Very limited vocabulary or frequently poor word choice.	No variety, persistent mistakes.	Enough errors to create confusion.
1	No response, no examples.	Unfocused, confusing progression of ideas.	Basic errors in vocabulary.	No variety, serious flaws.	Persistent errors that consistently obscure the meaning.

In your opinion, what is the weakest aspect of this essay? What can you do to improve?

What is the strongest aspect of this essay? How would you advise others to do as well?

Practice Essay

Plan and write an essay on the topic below. You will not be timed, but you should try to limit yourself to no more than 25 minutes. When you're finished with your essay, use the rubric to evaluate your essay.

> Think carefully about the issue presented in the following excerpt and the assignment below:
>
> Opportunity is missed by most people because it is dressed in overalls and looks like work.
> ~Thomas Edison
>
> **Assignment:** Do opportunities require work? Plan and write an essay in which you develop your point of view on this issue. Support your position with reasoning and examples taken from your reading, studies, experience, or observations.

Essay Scoring Rubric

Instructions for use: This rubric is based on the rubric used by College Board SAT Essay Graders. For each category, assign the essay a score between 1 and 6. The overall essay score should be the average of the scores from each category. For example, if an essay scores a 4 in three categories and a 3 in two categories, the overall score is a 4. Always round to the nearest whole number. Use this rubric to score your essay. Be honest with yourself! The more critical you are, the more you can improve!

Score	Response and Support	Organization	Language Choice	Sentence Structure	Grammar, Usage, & Mechanics
6	Insightful response with specific, concrete, and clearly relevant examples cited as support.	Clearly focused, smooth progression of ideas.	Varied, high level, and accurate vocabulary.	Substantial variety, few if any mistakes.	Very few and insignificant errors, if any.
5	Effective response, with fairly specific and generally relevant examples cited as support.	Focused, smooth progression of ideas.	Appropriate vocabulary.	Frequent variety, few mistakes.	More or less free of errors, errors do not interfere with meaning.
4	Response is there, but the examples aren't very specific or are entirely hypothetical and their relevance is barely adequate.	Generally focused, ideas progress but not very smoothly.	Adequate but inconsistent use of vocabulary.	Some variety, some mistakes.	Some errors.
3	Response is there, but the examples don't cut it.	Limited focus, ideas don't progress from one to another.	Weak vocabulary or occasionally poor word choice.	No variety, some mistakes.	A variety of errors.
2	Response is vague, and the examples are inappropriate or insufficient.	Poor focus, problems with progression of ideas.	Very limited vocabulary or frequently poor word choice.	No variety, persistent mistakes.	Enough errors to create confusion.
1	No response, no examples.	Unfocused, confusing progression of ideas.	Basic errors in vocabulary.	No variety, serious flaws.	Persistent errors that consistently obscure the meaning.

Version 1.3 Unauthorized copying or reuse of any part of this page is illegal.

In your opinion, what is the weakest aspect of this essay? What can you do to improve?

What is the strongest aspect of this essay? How would you advise others to do as well?

Red Essay 17

Practice Essay

Plan and write an essay on the topic below. You will not be timed, but you should try to limit yourself to no more than 25 minutes. When you're finished with your essay, use the rubric to evaluate your essay.

> Think carefully about the issue presented in the following excerpt and the assignment below:
>
> It's a poor sort of memory that only works backwards.
> ~Lewis Carroll
>
> **Assignment:** Which is more important when making decisions: learning from the past, or considering the future? Plan and write an essay in which you develop your point of view on this issue. Support your position with reasoning and examples taken from your reading, studies, experience, or observations.

Essay Scoring Rubric

Instructions for use: This rubric is based on the rubric used by College Board SAT Essay Graders. For each category, assign the essay a score between 1 and 6. The overall essay score should be the average of the scores from each category. For example, if an essay scores a 4 in three categories and a 3 in two categories, the overall score is a 4. Always round to the nearest whole number. Use this rubric to score your essay. Be honest with yourself! The more critical you are, the more you can improve!

Score	Response and Support	Organization	Language Choice	Sentence Structure	Grammar, Usage, & Mechanics
6	Insightful response with specific, concrete, and clearly relevant examples cited as support.	Clearly focused, smooth progression of ideas.	Varied, high level, and accurate vocabulary.	Substantial variety, few if any mistakes.	Very few and insignificant errors, if any.
5	Effective response, with fairly specific and generally relevant examples cited as support.	Focused, smooth progression of ideas.	Appropriate vocabulary.	Frequent variety, few mistakes.	More or less free of errors, errors do not interfere with meaning.
4	Response is there, but the examples aren't very specific or are entirely hypothetical and their relevance is barely adequate.	Generally focused, ideas progress but not very smoothly.	Adequate but inconsistent use of vocabulary.	Some variety, some mistakes.	Some errors.
3	Response is there, but the examples don't cut it.	Limited focus, ideas don't progress from one to another.	Weak vocabulary or occasionally poor word choice.	No variety, some mistakes.	A variety of errors.
2	Response is vague, and the examples are inappropriate or insufficient.	Poor focus, problems with progression of ideas.	Very limited vocabulary or frequently poor word choice.	No variety, persistent mistakes.	Enough errors to create confusion.
1	No response, no examples.	Unfocused, confusing progression of ideas.	Basic errors in vocabulary.	No variety, serious flaws.	Persistent errors that consistently obscure the meaning.

In your opinion, what is the weakest aspect of this essay? What can you do to improve?

___

What is the strongest aspect of this essay? How would you advise others to do as well?

___

Practice Essay

Plan and write an essay on the topic below. You will not be timed, but you should try to limit yourself to no more than 25 minutes. When you're finished with your essay, use the rubric to evaluate your essay.

> Think carefully about the issue presented in the following excerpt and the assignment below:
>
> A rock pile ceases to be a rock pile the moment a single man contemplates it, bearing within him the image of a cathedral.
> ~Antoine de Saint-Exupery
>
> **Assignment:** In your opinion, what role does creativity play in advancing civilization? Plan and write an essay in which you develop your point of view on this issue. Support your position with reasoning and examples taken from your reading, studies, experience, or observations.

Essay Scoring Rubric

Instructions for use: This rubric is based on the rubric used by College Board SAT Essay Graders. For each category, assign the essay a score between 1 and 6. The overall essay score should be the average of the scores from each category. For example, if an essay scores a 4 in three categories and a 3 in two categories, the overall score is a 4. Always round to the nearest whole number. Use this rubric to score your essay. Be honest with yourself! The more critical you are, the more you can improve!

Score	Response and Support	Organization	Language Choice	Sentence Structure	Grammar, Usage, & Mechanics
6	Insightful response with specific, concrete, and clearly relevant examples cited as support.	Clearly focused, smooth progression of ideas.	Varied, high level, and accurate vocabulary.	Substantial variety, few if any mistakes.	Very few and insignificant errors, if any.
5	Effective response, with fairly specific and generally relevant examples cited as support.	Focused, smooth progression of ideas.	Appropriate vocabulary.	Frequent variety, few mistakes.	More or less free of errors, errors do not interfere with meaning.
4	Response is there, but the examples aren't very specific or are entirely hypothetical and their relevance is barely adequate.	Generally focused, ideas progress but not very smoothly.	Adequate but inconsistent use of vocabulary.	Some variety, some mistakes.	Some errors.
3	Response is there, but the examples don't cut it.	Limited focus, ideas don't progress from one to another.	Weak vocabulary or occasionally poor word choice.	No variety, some mistakes.	A variety of errors.
2	Response is vague, and the examples are inappropriate or insufficient.	Poor focus, problems with progression of ideas.	Very limited vocabulary or frequently poor word choice.	No variety, persistent mistakes.	Enough errors to create confusion.
1	No response, no examples.	Unfocused, confusing progression of ideas.	Basic errors in vocabulary.	No variety, serious flaws.	Persistent errors that consistently obscure the meaning.

Version 1.3   Unauthorized copying or reuse of any part of this page is illegal.

In your opinion, what is the weakest aspect of this essay? What can you do to improve?

What is the strongest aspect of this essay? How would you advise others to do as well?

Practice Essay

Plan and write an essay on the topic below. You will not be timed, but you should try to limit yourself to no more than 25 minutes. When you're finished with your essay, use the rubric to evaluate your essay.

> Think carefully about the issue presented in the following excerpt and the assignment below:
>
> At the end of your life, you will never regret not having passed one more test, not winning one more verdict, or not closing one more deal. You will regret time not spent with a husband, a friend, a child, or a parent.
> ~Barbara Bush
>
> **Assignment:** Does society focus too much on "success" and not enough on family and relationships? Plan and write an essay in which you develop your point of view on this issue. Support your position with reasoning and examples taken from your reading, studies, experience, or observations.

Essay Scoring Rubric

Instructions for use: This rubric is based on the rubric used by College Board SAT Essay Graders. For each category, assign the essay a score between 1 and 6. The overall essay score should be the average of the scores from each category. For example, if an essay scores a 4 in three categories and a 3 in two categories, the overall score is a 4. Always round to the nearest whole number. Use this rubric to score your essay. Be honest with yourself! The more critical you are, the more you can improve!

Score	Response and Support	Organization	Language Choice	Sentence Structure	Grammar, Usage, & Mechanics
6	Insightful response with specific, concrete, and clearly relevant examples cited as support.	Clearly focused, smooth progression of ideas.	Varied, high level, and accurate vocabulary.	Substantial variety, few if any mistakes.	Very few and insignificant errors, if any.
5	Effective response, with fairly specific and generally relevant examples cited as support.	Focused, smooth progression of ideas.	Appropriate vocabulary.	Frequent variety, few mistakes.	More or less free of errors, errors do not interfere with meaning.
4	Response is there, but the examples aren't very specific or are entirely hypothetical and their relevance is barely adequate.	Generally focused, ideas progress but not very smoothly.	Adequate but inconsistent use of vocabulary.	Some variety, some mistakes.	Some errors.
3	Response is there, but the examples don't cut it.	Limited focus, ideas don't progress from one to another.	Weak vocabulary or occasionally poor word choice.	No variety, some mistakes.	A variety of errors.
2	Response is vague, and the examples are inappropriate or insufficient.	Poor focus, problems with progression of ideas.	Very limited vocabulary or frequently poor word choice.	No variety, persistent mistakes.	Enough errors to create confusion.
1	No response, no examples.	Unfocused, confusing progression of ideas.	Basic errors in vocabulary.	No variety, serious flaws.	Persistent errors that consistently obscure the meaning.

In your opinion, what is the weakest aspect of this essay? What can you do to improve?

What is the strongest aspect of this essay? How would you advise others to do as well?

Practice Essay

Plan and write an essay on the topic below. You will not be timed, but you should try to limit yourself to no more than 25 minutes. When you're finished with your essay, use the rubric to evaluate your essay.

> Think carefully about the issue presented in the following excerpt and the assignment below:
>
> It is questionable if all the mechanical inventions yet made have lightened the day's toil of any human being.
> ~John Stuart Mill
>
> **Assignment:** Has technology allowed people to work less today than in the past? Plan and write an essay in which you develop your point of view on this issue. Support your position with reasoning and examples taken from your reading, studies, experience, or observations.

Essay Scoring Rubric

Instructions for use: This rubric is based on the rubric used by College Board SAT Essay Graders. For each category, assign the essay a score between 1 and 6. The overall essay score should be the average of the scores from each category. For example, if an essay scores a 4 in three categories and a 3 in two categories, the overall score is a 4. Always round to the nearest whole number. Use this rubric to score your essay. Be honest with yourself! The more critical you are, the more you can improve!

Score	Response and Support	Organization	Language Choice	Sentence Structure	Grammar, Usage, & Mechanics
6	Insightful response with specific, concrete, and clearly relevant examples cited as support.	Clearly focused, smooth progression of ideas.	Varied, high level, and accurate vocabulary.	Substantial variety, few if any mistakes.	Very few and insignificant errors, if any.
5	Effective response, with fairly specific and generally relevant examples cited as support.	Focused, smooth progression of ideas.	Appropriate vocabulary.	Frequent variety, few mistakes.	More or less free of errors, errors do not interfere with meaning.
4	Response is there, but the examples aren't very specific or are entirely hypothetical and their relevance is barely adequate.	Generally focused, ideas progress but not very smoothly.	Adequate but inconsistent use of vocabulary.	Some variety, some mistakes.	Some errors.
3	Response is there, but the examples don't cut it.	Limited focus, ideas don't progress from one to another.	Weak vocabulary or occasionally poor word choice.	No variety, some mistakes.	A variety of errors.
2	Response is vague, and the examples are inappropriate or insufficient.	Poor focus, problems with progression of ideas.	Very limited vocabulary or frequently poor word choice.	No variety, persistent mistakes.	Enough errors to create confusion.
1	No response, no examples.	Unfocused, confusing progression of ideas.	Basic errors in vocabulary.	No variety, serious flaws.	Persistent errors that consistently obscure the meaning.

Version 1.3   Unauthorized copying or reuse of any part of this page is illegal.

In your opinion, what is the weakest aspect of this essay? What can you do to improve?

What is the strongest aspect of this essay? How would you advise others to do as well?

Red Essay 21

Practice Essay

Plan and write an essay on the topic below. You will not be timed, but you should try to limit yourself to no more than 25 minutes. When you're finished with your essay, use the rubric to evaluate your essay.

> Think carefully about the issue presented in the following excerpt and the assignment below:
>
> I owe my success to having listened respectfully to the very best advice, and
> then going away and doing the exact opposite.
> ~G.K. Chesterton
>
> **Assignment:** Are people held back by their adherence to the beliefs of the majority or to doing things in the conventional way? Plan and write an essay in which you develop your point of view on this issue. Support your position with reasoning and examples taken from your reading, studies, experience, or observations.

Essay Scoring Rubric

Instructions for use: This rubric is based on the rubric used by College Board SAT Essay Graders. For each category, assign the essay a score between 1 and 6. The overall essay score should be the average of the scores from each category. For example, if an essay scores a 4 in three categories and a 3 in two categories, the overall score is a 4. Always round to the nearest whole number. Use this rubric to score your essay. Be honest with yourself! The more critical you are, the more you can improve!

Score	Response and Support	Organization	Language Choice	Sentence Structure	Grammar, Usage, & Mechanics
6	Insightful response with specific, concrete, and clearly relevant examples cited as support.	Clearly focused, smooth progression of ideas.	Varied, high level, and accurate vocabulary.	Substantial variety, few if any mistakes.	Very few and insignificant errors, if any.
5	Effective response, with fairly specific and generally relevant examples cited as support.	Focused, smooth progression of ideas.	Appropriate vocabulary.	Frequent variety, few mistakes.	More or less free of errors, errors do not interfere with meaning.
4	Response is there, but the examples aren't very specific or are entirely hypothetical and their relevance is barely adequate.	Generally focused, ideas progress but not very smoothly.	Adequate but inconsistent use of vocabulary.	Some variety, some mistakes.	Some errors.
3	Response is there, but the examples don't cut it.	Limited focus, ideas don't progress from one to another.	Weak vocabulary or occasionally poor word choice.	No variety, some mistakes.	A variety of errors.
2	Response is vague, and the examples are inappropriate or insufficient.	Poor focus, problems with progression of ideas.	Very limited vocabulary or frequently poor word choice.	No variety, persistent mistakes.	Enough errors to create confusion.
1	No response, no examples.	Unfocused, confusing progression of ideas.	Basic errors in vocabulary.	No variety, serious flaws.	Persistent errors that consistently obscure the meaning.

Unauthorized copying or reuse of any part of this page is illegal.

Version 1.3

In your opinion, what is the weakest aspect of this essay? What can you do to improve?

____

What is the strongest aspect of this essay? How would you advise others to do as well?

____

Practice Essay

Plan and write an essay on the topic below. You will not be timed, but you should try to limit yourself to no more than 25 minutes. When you're finished with your essay, use the rubric to evaluate your essay.

> Think carefully about the issue presented in the following excerpt and the assignment below:
>
> Believe those who are seeking the truth. Doubt those who find it.
> ~Andre Gido
>
> **Assignment:** Is it possible to discover the truth, or is truth something that we must always seek but never truly find? Plan and write an essay in which you develop your point of view on this issue. Support your position with reasoning and examples taken from your reading, studies, experience, or observations.

Essay Scoring Rubric

Instructions for use: This rubric is based on the rubric used by College Board SAT Essay Graders. For each category, assign the essay a score between 1 and 6. The overall essay score should be the average of the scores from each category. For example, if an essay scores a 4 in three categories and a 3 in two categories, the overall score is a 4. Always round to the nearest whole number. Use this rubric to score your essay. Be honest with yourself! The more critical you are, the more you can improve!

Score	Response and Support	Organization	Language Choice	Sentence Structure	Grammar, Usage, & Mechanics
6	Insightful response with specific, concrete, and clearly relevant examples cited as support.	Clearly focused, smooth progression of ideas.	Varied, high level, and accurate vocabulary.	Substantial variety, few if any mistakes.	Very few and insignificant errors, if any.
5	Effective response, with fairly specific and generally relevant examples cited as support.	Focused, smooth progression of ideas.	Appropriate vocabulary.	Frequent variety, few mistakes.	More or less free of errors, errors do not interfere with meaning.
4	Response is there, but the examples aren't very specific or are entirely hypothetical and their relevance is barely adequate.	Generally focused, ideas progress but not very smoothly.	Adequate but inconsistent use of vocabulary.	Some variety, some mistakes.	Some errors.
3	Response is there, but the examples don't cut it.	Limited focus, ideas don't progress from one to another.	Weak vocabulary or occasionally poor word choice.	No variety, some mistakes.	A variety of errors.
2	Response is vague, and the examples are inappropriate or insufficient.	Poor focus, problems with progression of ideas.	Very limited vocabulary or frequently poor word choice.	No variety, persistent mistakes.	Enough errors to create confusion.
1	No response, no examples.	Unfocused, confusing progression of ideas.	Basic errors in vocabulary.	No variety, serious flaws.	Persistent errors that consistently obscure the meaning.

Version 1.3   Unauthorized copying or reuse of any part of this page is illegal.

In your opinion, what is the weakest aspect of this essay? What can you do to improve?

What is the strongest aspect of this essay? How would you advise others to do as well?

Red Essay 23

Practice Essay

Plan and write an essay on the topic below. You will not be timed, but you should try to limit yourself to no more than 25 minutes. When you're finished with your essay, use the rubric to evaluate your essay.

> Think carefully about the issue presented in the following excerpt and the assignment below:
>
> When the first Superman movie came out I was frequently asked "What is a hero?"...My answer was that a hero is someone who commits a courageous action without considering the consequences...Now my definition is completely different. I think a hero is an ordinary individual who finds strength to persevere and endure in spite of overwhelming obstacles.
> ~Christopher Reeve
>
> **Assignment:** What makes a hero: courage and bravery, or inner strength and perseverance? Plan and write an essay in which you develop your point of view on this issue. Support your position with reasoning and examples taken from your reading, studies, experience, or observations.

Essay Scoring Rubric

Instructions for use: This rubric is based on the rubric used by College Board SAT Essay Graders. For each category, assign the essay a score between 1 and 6. The overall essay score should be the average of the scores from each category. For example, if an essay scores a 4 in three categories and a 3 in two categories, the overall score is a 4. Always round to the nearest whole number. Use this rubric to score your essay. Be honest with yourself! The more critical you are, the more you can improve!

Score	Response and Support	Organization	Language Choice	Sentence Structure	Grammar, Usage, & Mechanics
6	Insightful response with specific, concrete, and clearly relevant examples cited as support.	Clearly focused, smooth progression of ideas.	Varied, high level, and accurate vocabulary.	Substantial variety, few if any mistakes.	Very few and insignificant errors, if any.
5	Effective response, with fairly specific and generally relevant examples cited as support.	Focused, smooth progression of ideas.	Appropriate vocabulary.	Frequent variety, few mistakes.	More or less free of errors, errors do not interfere with meaning.
4	Response is there, but the examples aren't very specific or are entirely hypothetical and their relevance is barely adequate.	Generally focused, ideas progress but not very smoothly.	Adequate but inconsistent use of vocabulary.	Some variety, some mistakes.	Some errors.
3	Response is there, but the examples don't cut it.	Limited focus, ideas don't progress from one to another.	Weak vocabulary or occasionally poor word choice.	No variety, some mistakes.	A variety of errors.
2	Response is vague, and the examples are inappropriate or insufficient.	Poor focus, problems with progression of ideas.	Very limited vocabulary or frequently poor word choice.	No variety, persistent mistakes.	Enough errors to create confusion.
1	No response, no examples.	Unfocused, confusing progression of ideas.	Basic errors in vocabulary.	No variety, serious flaws.	Persistent errors that consistently obscure the meaning.

In your opinion, what is the weakest aspect of this essay? What can you do to improve?

What is the strongest aspect of this essay? How would you advise others to do as well?

Practice Essay

Plan and write an essay on the topic below. You will not be timed, but you should try to limit yourself to no more than 25 minutes. When you're finished with your essay, use the rubric to evaluate your essay.

> Think carefully about the issue presented in the following excerpt and the assignment below:
>
> Many powerful leaders throughout history have considered themselves above the law and acted in ways that violated the laws or guidelines of their own country or group. People are quick to condemn these leaders, but shouldn't leaders be held to different standards? If what a leader is doing benefits the majority of the people in a country or group, then it does not matter if a law or guideline is violated.
>
> **Assignment:** Should a leader be above the law if his actions benefit the majority? Plan and write an essay in which you develop your point of view on this issue. Support your position with reasoning and examples taken from your reading, studies, experience, or observations.

Essay Scoring Rubric

Instructions for use: This rubric is based on the rubric used by College Board SAT Essay Graders. For each category, assign the essay a score between 1 and 6. The overall essay score should be the average of the scores from each category. For example, if an essay scores a 4 in three categories and a 3 in two categories, the overall score is a 4. Always round to the nearest whole number. Use this rubric to score your essay. Be honest with yourself! The more critical you are, the more you can improve!

Score	Response and Support	Organization	Language Choice	Sentence Structure	Grammar, Usage, & Mechanics
6	Insightful response with specific, concrete, and clearly relevant examples cited as support.	Clearly focused, smooth progression of ideas.	Varied, high level, and accurate vocabulary.	Substantial variety, few if any mistakes.	Very few and insignificant errors, if any.
5	Effective response, with fairly specific and generally relevant examples cited as support.	Focused, smooth progression of ideas.	Appropriate vocabulary.	Frequent variety, few mistakes.	More or less free of errors, errors do not interfere with meaning.
4	Response is there, but the examples aren't very specific or are entirely hypothetical and their relevance is barely adequate.	Generally focused, ideas progress but not very smoothly.	Adequate but inconsistent use of vocabulary.	Some variety, some mistakes.	Some errors.
3	Response is there, but the examples don't cut it.	Limited focus, ideas don't progress from one to another.	Weak vocabulary or occasionally poor word choice.	No variety, some mistakes.	A variety of errors.
2	Response is vague, and the examples are inappropriate or insufficient.	Poor focus, problems with progression of ideas.	Very limited vocabulary or frequently poor word choice.	No variety, persistent mistakes.	Enough errors to create confusion.
1	No response, no examples.	Unfocused, confusing progression of ideas.	Basic errors in vocabulary.	No variety, serious flaws.	Persistent errors that consistently obscure the meaning.

Version 1.3   Unauthorized copying or reuse of any part of this page is illegal.

In your opinion, what is the weakest aspect of this essay? What can you do to improve?

What is the strongest aspect of this essay? How would you advise others to do as well?

Red Essay 25

Practice Essay

Plan and write an essay on the topic below. You will not be timed, but you should try to limit yourself to no more than 25 minutes. When you're finished with your essay, use the rubric to evaluate your essay.

> Think carefully about the issue presented in the following excerpt and the assignment below:
>
> Destiny is not a matter of change, it is a matter of choice; it is not a thing to be waited for, it is a thing to be achieved.
> ~William Jennings Bryant
>
> **Assignment:** Do we create our own destinies or are they preordained? Plan and write an essay in which you develop your point of view on this issue. Support your position with reasoning and examples taken from your reading, studies, experience, or observations.

Essay Scoring Rubric

Instructions for use: This rubric is based on the rubric used by College Board SAT Essay Graders. For each category, assign the essay a score between 1 and 6. The overall essay score should be the average of the scores from each category. For example, if an essay scores a 4 in three categories and a 3 in two categories, the overall score is a 4. Always round to the nearest whole number. Use this rubric to score your essay. Be honest with yourself! The more critical you are, the more you can improve!

Score	Response and Support	Organization	Language Choice	Sentence Structure	Grammar, Usage, & Mechanics
6	Insightful response with specific, concrete, and clearly relevant examples cited as support.	Clearly focused, smooth progression of ideas.	Varied, high level, and accurate vocabulary.	Substantial variety, few if any mistakes.	Very few and insignificant errors, if any.
5	Effective response, with fairly specific and generally relevant examples cited as support.	Focused, smooth progression of ideas.	Appropriate vocabulary.	Frequent variety, few mistakes.	More or less free of errors, errors do not interfere with meaning.
4	Response is there, but the examples aren't very specific or are entirely hypothetical and their relevance is barely adequate.	Generally focused, ideas progress but not very smoothly.	Adequate but inconsistent use of vocabulary.	Some variety, some mistakes.	Some errors.
3	Response is there, but the examples don't cut it.	Limited focus, ideas don't progress from one to another.	Weak vocabulary or occasionally poor word choice.	No variety, some mistakes.	A variety of errors.
2	Response is vague, and the examples are inappropriate or insufficient.	Poor focus, problems with progression of ideas.	Very limited vocabulary or frequently poor word choice.	No variety, persistent mistakes.	Enough errors to create confusion.
1	No response, no examples.	Unfocused, confusing progression of ideas.	Basic errors in vocabulary.	No variety, serious flaws.	Persistent errors that consistently obscure the meaning.

In your opinion, what is the weakest aspect of this essay? What can you do to improve?

_____
_____
_____
_____
_____
_____
_____
_____
_____

What is the strongest aspect of this essay? How would you advise others to do as well?

_____
_____
_____
_____
_____
_____
_____
_____
_____

Practice Essay

Plan and write an essay on the topic below. You will not be timed, but you should try to limit yourself to no more than 25 minutes. When you're finished with your essay, use the rubric to evaluate your essay.

> Think carefully about the issue presented in the following excerpt and the assignment below:
>
> Here's to the crazy ones. The misfits. The rebels. The trouble-makers. The round pegs in the square holes. The ones who see things differently. They're not fond of rules, and they have no respect for the status-quo. You can quote them, disagree with them, glorify or vilify them. But the only thing you can't do is ignore them. Because they change things. They push the human race forward. And while some may see them as the crazy ones, we see genius. Because the people who are crazy enough to think they can change the world, are the ones who do.
>
> **Assignment:** Do you agree that it is the "rebels" of society who create the most change? Plan and write an essay in which you develop your point of view on this issue. Support your position with reasoning and examples taken from your reading, studies, experience, or observations.

Essay Scoring Rubric

Instructions for use: This rubric is based on the rubric used by College Board SAT Essay Graders. For each category, assign the essay a score between 1 and 6. The overall essay score should be the average of the scores from each category. For example, if an essay scores a 4 in three categories and a 3 in two categories, the overall score is a 4. Always round to the nearest whole number. Use this rubric to score your essay. Be honest with yourself! The more critical you are, the more you can improve!

Score	Response and Support	Organization	Language Choice	Sentence Structure	Grammar, Usage, & Mechanics
6	Insightful response with specific, concrete, and clearly relevant examples cited as support.	Clearly focused, smooth progression of ideas.	Varied, high level, and accurate vocabulary.	Substantial variety, few if any mistakes.	Very few and insignificant errors, if any.
5	Effective response, with fairly specific and generally relevant examples cited as support.	Focused, smooth progression of ideas.	Appropriate vocabulary.	Frequent variety, few mistakes.	More or less free of errors, errors do not interfere with meaning.
4	Response is there, but the examples aren't very specific or are entirely hypothetical and their relevance is barely adequate.	Generally focused, ideas progress but not very smoothly.	Adequate but inconsistent use of vocabulary.	Some variety, some mistakes.	Some errors.
3	Response is there, but the examples don't cut it.	Limited focus, ideas don't progress from one to another.	Weak vocabulary or occasionally poor word choice.	No variety, some mistakes.	A variety of errors.
2	Response is vague, and the examples are inappropriate or insufficient.	Poor focus, problems with progression of ideas.	Very limited vocabulary or frequently poor word choice.	No variety, persistent mistakes.	Enough errors to create confusion.
1	No response, no examples.	Unfocused, confusing progression of ideas.	Basic errors in vocabulary.	No variety, serious flaws.	Persistent errors that consistently obscure the meaning.

Version 1.3   Unauthorized copying or reuse of any part of this page is illegal.

In your opinion, what is the weakest aspect of this essay? What can you do to improve?

What is the strongest aspect of this essay? How would you advise others to do as well?

Red Essay 27

Practice Essay

Plan and write an essay on the topic below. You will not be timed, but you should try to limit yourself to no more than 25 minutes. When you're finished with your essay, use the rubric to evaluate your essay.

> Think carefully about the issue presented in the following excerpt and the assignment below:
>
> When a man sits with a pretty girl for an hour, it seems like a minute. But let him sit on a host stove for a minute – and it's longer than any hour. That's relativity.
> ~Albert Einstein
>
> **Assignment:** Do circumstances change the way we perceive things? Plan and write an essay in which you develop your point of view on this issue. Support your position with reasoning and examples taken from your reading, studies, experience, or observations.

Essay Scoring Rubric

Instructions for use: This rubric is based on the rubric used by College Board SAT Essay Graders. For each category, assign the essay a score between 1 and 6. The overall essay score should be the average of the scores from each category. For example, if an essay scores a 4 in three categories and a 3 in two categories, the overall score is a 4. Always round to the nearest whole number. Use this rubric to score your essay. Be honest with yourself! The more critical you are, the more you can improve!

Score	Response and Support	Organization	Language Choice	Sentence Structure	Grammar, Usage, & Mechanics
6	Insightful response with specific, concrete, and clearly relevant examples cited as support.	Clearly focused, smooth progression of ideas.	Varied, high level, and accurate vocabulary.	Substantial variety, few if any mistakes.	Very few and insignificant errors, if any.
5	Effective response, with fairly specific and generally relevant examples cited as support.	Focused, smooth progression of ideas.	Appropriate vocabulary.	Frequent variety, few mistakes.	More or less free of errors, errors do not interfere with meaning.
4	Response is there, but the examples aren't very specific or are entirely hypothetical and their relevance is barely adequate.	Generally focused, ideas progress but not very smoothly.	Adequate but inconsistent use of vocabulary.	Some variety, some mistakes.	Some errors.
3	Response is there, but the examples don't cut it.	Limited focus, ideas don't progress from one to another.	Weak vocabulary or occasionally poor word choice.	No variety, some mistakes.	A variety of errors.
2	Response is vague, and the examples are inappropriate or insufficient.	Poor focus, problems with progression of ideas.	Very limited vocabulary or frequently poor word choice.	No variety, persistent mistakes.	Enough errors to create confusion.
1	No response, no examples.	Unfocused, confusing progression of ideas.	Basic errors in vocabulary.	No variety, serious flaws.	Persistent errors that consistently obscure the meaning.

In your opinion, what is the weakest aspect of this essay? What can you do to improve?

What is the strongest aspect of this essay? How would you advise others to do as well?

Practice Essay

Plan and write an essay on the topic below. You will not be timed, but you should try to limit yourself to no more than 25 minutes. When you're finished with your essay, use the rubric to evaluate your essay.

> Think carefully about the issue presented in the following excerpt and the assignment below:
>
> > Genuine tragedies in the world are not conflicts between right and wrong. They are conflicts between two rights. ~Anonymous
>
> **Assignment:** Can both parties in a conflict be right, or must there always be a right side and a wrong side? Plan and write an essay in which you develop your point of view on this issue. Support your position with reasoning and examples taken from your reading, studies, experience, or observations.

Essay Scoring Rubric

Instructions for use: This rubric is based on the rubric used by College Board SAT Essay Graders. For each category, assign the essay a score between 1 and 6. The overall essay score should be the average of the scores from each category. For example, if an essay scores a 4 in three categories and a 3 in two categories, the overall score is a 4. Always round to the nearest whole number. Use this rubric to score your essay. Be honest with yourself! The more critical you are, the more you can improve!

Score	Response and Support	Organization	Language Choice	Sentence Structure	Grammar, Usage, & Mechanics
6	Insightful response with specific, concrete, and clearly relevant examples cited as support.	Clearly focused, smooth progression of ideas.	Varied, high level, and accurate vocabulary.	Substantial variety, few if any mistakes.	Very few and insignificant errors, if any.
5	Effective response, with fairly specific and generally relevant examples cited as support.	Focused, smooth progression of ideas.	Appropriate vocabulary.	Frequent variety, few mistakes.	More or less free of errors, errors do not interfere with meaning.
4	Response is there, but the examples aren't very specific or are entirely hypothetical and their relevance is barely adequate.	Generally focused, ideas progress but not very smoothly.	Adequate but inconsistent use of vocabulary.	Some variety, some mistakes.	Some errors.
3	Response is there, but the examples don't cut it.	Limited focus, ideas don't progress from one to another.	Weak vocabulary or occasionally poor word choice.	No variety, some mistakes.	A variety of errors.
2	Response is vague, and the examples are inappropriate or insufficient.	Poor focus, problems with progression of ideas.	Very limited vocabulary or frequently poor word choice.	No variety, persistent mistakes.	Enough errors to create confusion.
1	No response, no examples.	Unfocused, confusing progression of ideas.	Basic errors in vocabulary.	No variety, serious flaws.	Persistent errors that consistently obscure the meaning.

Version 1.3   Unauthorized copying or reuse of any part of this page is illegal.

In your opinion, what is the weakest aspect of this essay? What can you do to improve?

What is the strongest aspect of this essay? How would you advise others to do as well?

Red Essay 29

Practice Essay

Plan and write an essay on the topic below. You will not be timed, but you should try to limit yourself to no more than 25 minutes. When you're finished with your essay, use the rubric to evaluate your essay.

> Think carefully about the issue presented in the following excerpt and the assignment below:
>
> In general people experience their present naively, as it were, without being able to form an estimate of its contents; they have first to put themselves at a distance from it – the present, that is to say, must have become the past – before it can yield points of vantage from which to judge the future.
> ~Sigmund Freud
>
> **Assignment:** Is it necessary for time to pass before we can appreciate or learn from our experiences? Plan and write an essay in which you develop your point of view on this issue. Support your position with reasoning and examples taken from your reading, studies, experience, or observations.

Red Essay 1

SAT Essay Basics

The College Board added the writing portion to the SAT in 2005 because many colleges complained about the lack of examples of a student's writing ability. The writing section, worth 800 points of the total test score, is made up of two parts: The essay and the multiple choice sections. The multiple choice counts for roughly 70% of your total writing score – the rest of your score is based on the essay.

This means that a perfect essay score could count for almost 170 points of your overall SAT score.

Even if you've read the College Board website, it can be very difficult to figure out exactly what the essay graders are looking for in a "perfect" essay. Because the College Board's essay grading rubric is very vague, there doesn't seem to be a simple checklist of things an essay must have in order to receive a six.

In the space below, make a list of things that you think an SAT essay has to have in order to receive a perfect score.

- _____
- _____
- _____
- _____
- _____
- _____

Essay Scoring Rubric

Instructions for use: This rubric is based on the rubric used by College Board SAT Essay Graders. For each category, assign the essay a score between 1 and 6. The overall essay score should be the average of the scores from each category. For example, if an essay scores a 4 in three categories and a 3 in two categories, the overall score is a 4. Always round to the nearest whole number. Use this rubric to score your essay. Be honest with yourself! The more critical you are, the more you can improve!

Score	Response and Support	Organization	Language Choice	Sentence Structure	Grammar, Usage, & Mechanics
6	Insightful response with specific, concrete, and clearly relevant examples cited as support.	Clearly focused, smooth progression of ideas.	Varied, high level, and accurate vocabulary.	Substantial variety, few if any mistakes.	Very few and insignificant errors, if any.
5	Effective response, with fairly specific and generally relevant examples cited as support.	Focused, smooth progression of ideas.	Appropriate vocabulary.	Frequent variety, few mistakes.	More or less free of errors, errors do not interfere with meaning.
4	Response is there, but the examples aren't very specific or are entirely hypothetical and their relevance is barely adequate.	Generally focused, ideas progress but not very smoothly.	Adequate but inconsistent use of vocabulary.	Some variety, some mistakes.	Some errors.
3	Response is there, but the examples don't cut it.	Limited focus, ideas don't progress from one to another.	Weak vocabulary or occasionally poor word choice.	No variety, some mistakes.	A variety of errors.
2	Response is vague, and the examples are inappropriate or insufficient.	Poor focus, problems with progression of ideas.	Very limited vocabulary or frequently poor word choice.	No variety, persistent mistakes.	Enough errors to create confusion.
1	No response, no examples.	Unfocused, confusing progression of ideas.	Basic errors in vocabulary.	No variety, serious flaws.	Persistent errors that consistently obscure the meaning.

In your opinion, what is the weakest aspect of this essay? What can you do to improve?

_____
_____
_____
_____
_____
_____
_____
_____

What is the strongest aspect of this essay? How would you advise others to do as well?

_____
_____
_____
_____
_____
_____
_____
_____
_____

Red Essay 30

Practice Essay

Plan and write an essay on the topic below. You will not be timed, but you should try to limit yourself to no more than 25 minutes. When you're finished with your essay, use the rubric to evaluate your essay.

> Think carefully about the issue presented in the following excerpt and the assignment below:
>
> The peculiar evil of silencing the expression of an opinion is that it is robbing the human race; posterity as well as the existing generation; those who dissent from the opinion still more than those who hold it. If the opinion is right, they are deprived of the opportunity of exchanging error for truth; if wrong, they lose what is almost as great a benefit, the clearer perception and livelier impression of truth, produced by its collision with error.
> ~John Stuart Mill
>
> **Assignment:** Is it ever okay to limit free speech? Plan and write an essay in which you develop your point of view on this issue. Support your position with reasoning and examples taken from your reading, studies, experience, or observations.

Essay Scoring Rubric

Instructions for use: This rubric is based on the rubric used by College Board SAT Essay Graders. For each category, assign the essay a score between 1 and 6. The overall essay score should be the average of the scores from each category. For example, if an essay scores a 4 in three categories and a 3 in two categories, the overall score is a 4. Always round to the nearest whole number. Use this rubric to score your essay. Be honest with yourself! The more critical you are, the more you can improve!

Score	Response and Support	Organization	Language Choice	Sentence Structure	Grammar, Usage, & Mechanics
6	Insightful response with specific, concrete, and clearly relevant examples cited as support.	Clearly focused, smooth progression of ideas.	Varied, high level, and accurate vocabulary.	Substantial variety, few if any mistakes.	Very few and insignificant errors, if any.
5	Effective response, with fairly specific and generally relevant examples cited as support.	Focused, smooth progression of ideas.	Appropriate vocabulary.	Frequent variety, few mistakes.	More or less free of errors, errors do not interfere with meaning.
4	Response is there, but the examples aren't very specific or are entirely hypothetical and their relevance is barely adequate.	Generally focused, ideas progress but not very smoothly.	Adequate but inconsistent use of vocabulary.	Some variety, some mistakes.	Some errors.
3	Response is there, but the examples don't cut it.	Limited focus, ideas don't progress from one to another.	Weak vocabulary or occasionally poor word choice.	No variety, some mistakes.	A variety of errors.
2	Response is vague, and the examples are inappropriate or insufficient.	Poor focus, problems with progression of ideas.	Very limited vocabulary or frequently poor word choice.	No variety, persistent mistakes.	Enough errors to create confusion.
1	No response, no examples.	Unfocused, confusing progression of ideas.	Basic errors in vocabulary.	No variety, serious flaws.	Persistent errors that consistently obscure the meaning.

Version 1.3   Unauthorized copying or reuse of any part of this page is illegal.

In your opinion, what is the weakest aspect of this essay? What can you do to improve?

What is the strongest aspect of this essay? How would you advise others to do as well?

Made in the USA
San Bernardino, CA
09 August 2015